SUPPLY CHAIN ANALYTICS

Hayden Van Der Post

Reactive Publishing

CONTENTS

Title Page

Chapter 1: Introduction to Supply Chain Analytics   1

Chapter 2: Data Management in Supply Chain Analytics   23

Chapter 3: Demand Forecasting and Planning   48

Chapter 4: Supply Chain Optimization   79

Chapter 5: Supply Chain Visibility and Monitoring   105

Chapter 6: Supplier Relationship and Risk Management   130

Chapter 7: Lean and Agile Supply Chains   156

Chapter 8: Customer-Centric Supply Chain Analytics   187

Chapter 9: Advanced Technologies in Supply Chain Analytics   211

Chapter 10: Implementing Analytics Projects in Supply Chains   239

Additional Resources   262

CHAPTER 1: INTRODUCTION TO SUPPLY CHAIN ANALYTICS

Defining Supply Chain Analytics

Within the intricate web of global trade and commerce, the term 'Supply Chain Analytics' emerges as a beacon, guiding enterprises through the complexities of sourcing, manufacturing, distribution, and delivery. At its core, Supply Chain Analytics represents the confluence of data analysis and business intelligence applied to supply chain activities, aimed at improving efficiency and creating a competitive advantage.

The essence of Supply Chain Analytics is enshrined in the meticulous examination of data to discern patterns, predict outcomes, and prescribe actions. It is an investigative process, one that delves into the vast troves of data generated across the supply chain to unlock insights that can drive strategic decisions. From the procurement of raw materials to the delivery of finished goods, every step generates valuable data that, when analyzed, can reveal opportunities for optimization.

This analytical discipline encompasses various tools and methodologies, ranging from fundamental descriptive statistics that summarize current supply chain conditions, to sophisticated machine learning algorithms capable of forecasting future trends. The objective is not merely to understand the present state but to anticipate the future, enabling proactive decision-making.

In leveraging Supply Chain Analytics, businesses can achieve a multitude of outcomes. They can reduce costs by identifying inefficiencies, forecast demand with greater accuracy, enhance customer satisfaction through improved service levels, and mitigate risks by recognizing potential disruptions before they occur. The power of analytics lies in its ability to transform raw data into actionable intelligence.

To elucidate the concept with a practical example, consider the application of predictive analytics in inventory management. By analyzing historical sales data, seasonal trends, and current market conditions, a predictive model can estimate future product demand. This foresight allows organizations to optimize inventory levels, reducing the risk of stockouts or excessive overstock, which in turn can lead to cost savings and increased sales.

As businesses continue to navigate an ever-changing landscape, the role of Supply Chain Analytics becomes increasingly vital. It is the compass that directs companies towards efficiency, resilience, and ultimately, sustainability. In the subsequent sections, we will explore the various types of analytics, the key performance indicators vital for supply chain health, and the challenges and triumphs faced when implementing analytics in a supply chain context.

Evolution of Supply Chain Management

Tracing the lineage of supply chain management provides a panorama of innovation, adaptation, and at times, revolution. The evolution of supply chain management is a chronicle of the human pursuit of efficiency and responsiveness in the face of ever-shifting market demands and technological advancements.

In the nascent stages of industrialization, supply chains were relatively simple and linear. Producers and consumers often existed within close proximity, and the flow of goods was straightforward. However, as industries expanded and markets globalized, the supply chain sprawled into a complex network of interactions. This complexity required new management approaches and sparked the initial flame of what would become supply chain management as we know it today.

The mid-20th century bore witness to a significant milestone in this evolution with the popularization of the Toyota Production System. This system introduced the world to 'Just-In-Time' (JIT) manufacturing, which emphasized the importance of reducing waste and improving quality. The JIT philosophy sought to produce and deliver products in precise quantities and at the exact needed time, thus minimizing inventory levels and fostering a nimble supply chain.

As the digital age dawned, information technology became the great enabler for supply chain management. The introduction of Enterprise Resource Planning (ERP) systems in the 1990s allowed for an unprecedented level of coordination and data sharing across different components of the supply chain. These systems became the backbone of supply chain operations, integrating processes from procurement to production to distribution under a single umbrella.

The turn of the millennium heralded the era of e-commerce, reshaping consumer expectations and, by extension, supply chain strategies. The demand for greater speed, transparency, and customization spurred the development of more sophisticated supply chain models. Companies began to adopt a more holistic approach, recognizing the interdependencies within their supply chains and the need for collaboration among suppliers, manufacturers, and retailers.

The latest chapter in this journey is being penned by the advent of Supply Chain 4.0, marked by the integration of advanced technologies such as the Internet of Things (IoT), artificial intelligence (AI), and blockchain. These technologies hold the promise of end-to-end visibility, predictive capabilities, and a level of automation previously unattainable. They are transforming supply chains into dynamic, interconnected systems that can learn, adapt, and optimize themselves in real-time.

Reflecting on this historical tapestry, one can appreciate the ever-evolving nature of supply chain management. From rudimentary beginnings to a sophisticated, tech-driven discipline, it has become clear that adaptability and continuous improvement are the cornerstones of effective supply chain management.

As we delve deeper into the specifics of Supply Chain Analytics in the following sections, we will build upon this historical foundation to understand how analytics not only fits into this evolution but also propels it forward. Through the lens of data and technology, we will explore how modern supply chains are being reimagined and what the future may hold for this essential facet of global commerce.

The Role of Analytics in Modern Supply Chains

In the intricate web of modern supply chains, the role of analytics emerges as the linchpin that holds together the promise of data-driven decision-making. Gone are the days when gut feelings and heuristic methods were the primary decision drivers. Today, analytics is the compass that guides supply chain professionals through a sea of data towards the shores of strategic insights and operational excellence.

The application of analytics in supply chains transcends traditional reporting; it is about harnessing the power of data to glean insights that inform better business decisions. Analytics provides a multifaceted lens through which supply chain managers can scrutinize every aspect of their operations—from procurement to product delivery, and beyond.

Descriptive analytics offers a retrospective view, analyzing historical data to answer what happened within a supply chain. This foundational analytic type paints a picture of past performance, enabling managers to identify patterns, trends, and variances. Think of it as the supply chain's rearview mirror, reflecting the results of actions already taken.

However, to navigate today's dynamic business environment, merely looking backwards is insufficient. Predictive analytics comes into play, utilizing statistical models and machine learning algorithms to forecast future scenarios. This forward-looking approach empowers businesses to anticipate demand, manage inventory levels proactively, and mitigate potential risks. It's akin to a supply chain's GPS system, offering routes to future destinations based on current conditions and historical data.

Prescriptive analytics goes a step further by not only predicting what could happen but also suggesting actions to achieve desired outcomes. It leverages optimization models and simulation to provide recommendations on the best course of action, considering numerous variables and constraints. This level of analytics acts as the supply chain's autopilot, charting the course to efficiency and effectiveness.

The role of analytics is also paramount in enhancing the customer experience. By analyzing customer data, businesses can tailor their supply chain strategies to meet individual preferences and expectations. This bespoke approach leads to higher customer satisfaction and loyalty, which are crucial in an era where the customer is king.

Analytics also serves as a risk management tool by identifying vulnerabilities within the supply chain. By analyzing data from various sources, companies can predict and prepare for disruptions, whether they be natural disasters, market volatility, or supplier instability. This proactive stance on risk management is not just about averting crises—it's about building resilient supply chains that can bend but not break under pressure.

Furthermore, analytics drives sustainability in supply chains by identifying areas where resources can be optimized, waste can be reduced, and environmental impact can be minimized. It's an instrument for aligning supply chain practices with the broader goals of corporate social responsibility and environmental stewardship.

As we dissect the role of analytics in each component of the supply chain, we will uncover the myriad ways in which data transforms operations. From enhancing visibility to driving innovation, analytics is the catalyst that propels supply chains into the future—a future where every decision is informed, every risk is calculated, and every opportunity is seized.

Types of Supply Chain Analytics (Descriptive, Predictive, Prescriptive)

Within the domain of supply chain analytics, three distinct types crystallize as the core methodologies by which data is transformed into actionable intelligence: descriptive, predictive, and prescriptive analytics. Each serves a unique purpose and, when combined, they form a comprehensive analytics strategy that can dramatically enhance supply chain performance.

Descriptive analytics is the most traditional form of analytics, focusing on the interpretation of historical data to identify patterns and trends. It answers the question, "What has happened?" by dissecting past events and outcomes. Tools commonly used in descriptive analytics include data aggregation and mining, along with various visualization techniques such as dashboards and heat maps.

In the sphere of supply chain management, descriptive analytics can unveil the performance of various processes and identify areas for improvement. For instance, it can highlight bottlenecks in logistics operations or pinpoint recurring issues with certain suppliers. These insights are invaluable for understanding the current state of the supply chain and serve as the empirical bedrock upon which further analysis is built.

Predictive Analytics: The Science of Foreseeing the Future

Predictive analytics takes a leap into the future. It uses a combination of historical data, statistical algorithms, and machine learning techniques to forecast what is likely to happen. The tools of the predictive analytics trade range from simple regression models to complex neural networks, each varying in sophistication and applicability.

In practice, predictive analytics can forecast demand for products, anticipate inventory shortages, and predict the potential impact of external factors such as economic shifts or weather disruptions. For example, a predictive model might analyze seasonal sales patterns to determine optimal stock levels for different times of the year, thereby improving inventory turnover rates and reducing carrying costs.

Prescriptive Analytics: The Strategy of Decision Optimization

Prescriptive analytics is where data science meets decision science. It not only predicts outcomes but also prescribes actions to achieve specific objectives. Optimization and simulation are the keystones of prescriptive analytics. These techniques consider a wide array of variables and constraints to suggest the best course of action among various alternatives.

In the context of supply chains, prescriptive analytics could recommend the most efficient delivery routes, or it could simulate the impact of implementing a new supply chain strategy before actual deployment. It can also advise on the best responses to forecasted demand changes, ensuring that supply chain agility is maintained.

The collective force of descriptive, predictive, and prescriptive analytics equips supply chain managers with a deep and nuanced understanding of their operations. Descriptive analytics provides the clarity of hindsight, predictive analytics offers foresight, and prescriptive analytics delivers actionable insight. Together, they enable a proactive approach to supply chain management that can mitigate risks, reduce costs, and increase customer satisfaction.

Key Performance Indicators (KPIs) in Supply Chain Analytics

The lifeblood of any robust analytics system is the Key Performance Indicators (KPIs) that provide measurable values reflecting the performance of business operations. In the realm of supply chain analytics, KPIs serve as the navigational beacons that guide decision-makers toward operational excellence and strategic prowess.

A myriad of KPIs exists, each tailored to offer insights into different facets of the supply chain. They range from financial metrics to service level indicators, from inventory measures to quality assessments. The selection of KPIs is crucial; they must align with the overall business strategy and enable leaders to track progress towards key objectives.

Financial KPIs are paramount in understanding the cost implications of supply chain activities. They typically include metrics such as 'Cost of Goods Sold' (COGS), 'Cash-to-Cash Cycle Time', and 'Freight Cost per Unit'. Monitoring these KPIs helps in controlling expenses, optimizing cash flow, and ensuring that the supply chain contributes positively to the bottom line.

Service KPIs focus on evaluating the delivery aspects of the supply chain. 'Order Fulfillment Cycle Time', 'On-time Delivery Rate', and 'Perfect Order Rate' are examples of service KPIs that reflect the ability to meet customer expectations. High performance in these KPIs is often correlated with increased customer loyalty and market share.

Inventory KPIs provide insights into the efficiency of inventory management. 'Days of Inventory On Hand' (DOH), 'Inventory Turnover', and 'Obsolete Inventory Percentage' are critical measures that indicate how well inventory is being managed. Effective inventory KPIs help in reducing carrying costs, freeing up working capital, and ensuring product availability.

Quality KPIs assess the reliability and excellence of supply chain operations. Metrics such as 'Return Rate', 'Defects Per Million Opportunities' (DPMO), and 'Supplier Quality Rating' gauge the integrity of products and the performance of suppliers. Mastery over quality KPIs can lead to superior products, fewer customer complaints, and a stronger reputation.

To harness the full potential of KPIs, they must be integrated into the daily operations and strategic planning of the supply chain. Dashboards and analytics platforms can bring these KPIs to life, providing real-time visibility and enabling swift reactions to emerging trends or issues. Moreover, KPIs can be instrumental in setting benchmarks, fostering continuous improvement, and driving competitive differentiation.

The interconnectivity between KPIs and the types of analytics previously discussed is clear. Descriptive analytics can help in understanding the 'what' and 'why' behind KPI performances. Predictive analytics can forecast future KPI trends, enabling preemptive action. Prescriptive analytics can suggest optimal decisions to improve KPI outcomes.

KPIs in Action: An Illustrative Example

To illustrate the practical application of KPIs, let's consider a hypothetical scenario involving 'On-time Delivery Rate'. A company notices a decline in this KPI over several quarters. Using descriptive analytics, they uncover that a recurring cause is delays in supplier shipments. Predictive analytics might further reveal that these delays are likely to worsen due to seasonal demand spikes. Armed with this foresight, the company can employ prescriptive analytics to explore alternative supplier strategies or adjust inventory levels, thereby improving the 'On-time Delivery Rate'.

In the following chapters, we will explore each category of KPIs in depth, examining their implications and demonstrating how to optimize them through strategic analytics initiatives. By mastering KPIs, supply chain leaders can craft a narrative of success, driving their operations toward efficiency, responsiveness, and innovation.

Data Sources for Supply Chain Analytics

Sourcing the right data is like embarking on a quest for the Holy Grail in the vast kingdom of supply chain management. It's a vital endeavor that underpins the efficacy of all analytical exercises. Data sources for supply chain analytics are the wellsprings from which insights and foresights flow, powering the decision-making processes that drive supply chain optimization.

Supply chain analytics draws from a rich tapestry of data sources, each contributing a unique thread to the analytical narrative. The data landscape is extensive, encompassing internal databases, supplier statistics, market trends, and customer feedback. Together, they form a comprehensive picture of the supply chain ecosystem.

Internal Data: The Organizational Chronicles

Internal data sources are the foundation of supply chain analytics. They include transactional data from Enterprise Resource Planning (ERP) systems, Warehouse Management Systems (WMS), and Customer Relationship Management (CRM) platforms. This data provides granular details on production, inventory levels, order fulfillment, and customer interactions.

Supplier Data: The Collaborative Compass

Supplier data is essential for a 360-degree view of the supply chain. It involves sharing and integration of data from various suppliers' systems, encompassing lead times, quality metrics, and delivery schedules. Collaborative platforms and Vendor Managed Inventory (VMI) systems facilitate the exchange of this data, enhancing visibility and coordination.

Market Data: The External Barometer

Market data offers context and benchmarking capabilities, presenting a broader perspective on industry trends, commodity prices, and economic indicators. Sources such as market research reports, trade associations, and governmental databases are invaluable for understanding the macroeconomic environment and competitive landscape.

Customer Data: The End-User Encyclopedia

Customer data is a treasure trove of insights into buyer behavior, preferences, and satisfaction levels. Point-of-Sale (POS) systems, e-commerce analytics, and social media monitoring tools are some channels through which this data is collected. It helps in tailoring supply chain strategies to meet customer demands more effectively.

IoT Data: The Sensory Network

Internet of Things (IoT) devices are revolutionizing data collection in the supply chain. Sensors on containers, pallets, and products provide real-time tracking and condition monitoring. This IoT-generated data is crucial for proactive management and predictive analytics, enabling interventions before potential issues escalate.

Unstructured Data: The Qualitative Quandary

Unstructured data, such as emails, call center transcripts, and maintenance logs, holds qualitative insights that are often untapped. Natural Language Processing (NLP) and text analytics techniques are required to extract meaning from this data, revealing patterns and sentiments that can inform customer service improvements and process optimization.

The true power of these data sources is unleashed when they are integrated and analyzed holistically. Data warehousing, data lakes, and advanced analytics platforms facilitate the consolidation of disparate data sets, allowing supply chain managers to derive comprehensive insights. The fusion of these data streams enables predictive modeling, risk assessment, and scenario planning.

With great data comes great responsibility. Data governance ensures the quality, security, and ethical use of data. It involves establishing policies and procedures around data access, classification, and lifecycle management. A robust data governance framework is essential for maintaining the integrity and reliability of the data sources that feed into supply chain analytics.

As we delve deeper into the intricacies of supply chain analytics, the importance of diverse, high-quality data sources cannot be overstated. They are the lifeblood of the analytical processes that inform strategic decision-making.

Challenges in Implementing Supply Chain Analytics

While the integration of analytics into supply chain management offers a multitude of benefits, it does not come without its challenges. The path to a fully analytical approach is fraught with obstacles that must be navigated carefully. These challenges range from technical and infrastructural issues to human factors and organizational culture.

One of the primary obstacles is the technical complexity inherent in supply chain analytics. The sheer volume of data, coupled with the need for advanced analytical tools and techniques, can be daunting. Supply chains are often sprawling networks, and integrating data across diverse systems and platforms—each with its own structure and format—presents significant difficulties.

The old adage 'garbage in, garbage out' is particularly pertinent here. The quality of the data being analyzed is crucial.

Inconsistent data, inaccuracies, and missing information can lead to flawed analyses and misguided decisions. Ensuring data integrity is complicated by the variety of sources and the need for data to be current and relevant.

Infrastructure and Resource Constraints

Infrastructure limitations are another common hurdle. The hardware and software necessary for effective supply chain analytics require investment, something organizations may be hesitant to commit to without a clear understanding of the potential ROI. Additionally, maintenance of this infrastructure and the scaling of resources to keep pace with growing data sets can strain budgets.

The talent gap in data analytics is a well-documented issue. Supply chain analytics requires a blend of skills: proficiency in data science, understanding of supply chain operations, and the business acumen to translate insights into action. Finding individuals with this combination of expertise is challenging, and training existing employees is a time and resource-intensive alternative.

Organizational culture can also be resistant to the data-driven transformation required for supply chain analytics. Employees accustomed to traditional decision-making processes may be skeptical of analytics, perceiving it as a threat to their expertise or job security. Overcoming this resistance requires a change management strategy that emphasizes the value of analytics and involves stakeholders at all levels.

Data security and privacy are paramount, particularly given the sensitivity of supply chain information. Protecting against breaches and ensuring compliance with an ever-evolving landscape of regulations is a constant challenge for organizations. The risks are compounded when collaborating with suppliers and partners, each of which may have different security standards.

The rapid pace of technological change means that today's cutting-edge analytics platforms may quickly become outdated. Staying abreast of developments in AI, machine learning, and other emerging technologies—and understanding how to leverage them effectively for supply chain analytics—is an ongoing challenge.

Lastly, the ultimate goal of supply chain analytics is to draw actionable insights that can lead to improved performance. However, translating complex data into clear, actionable strategies is not straightforward. It requires a nuanced understanding of the business, the supply chain, and the competitive landscape.

Despite these challenges, the potential rewards for successfully implementing supply chain analytics are substantial. Organizations that navigate these obstacles effectively can gain deeper insights into their operations, make more informed decisions, and ultimately achieve a competitive advantage.

Example Of Successful Supply Chain Analytics

In this section, we explore various case studies that exemplify the successful application of supply chain analytics. Each case study highlights the practical use of analytics to solve real-world supply chain problems, demonstrating the transformative power of data-driven decision-making.

A leading global retailer utilized predictive analytics to optimize its inventory levels. By analyzing historical sales data, weather patterns, and promotional calendars, the company developed a model that accurately forecasted demand for various products. This allowed the retailer to adjust inventory levels dynamically, reducing stockouts and overstock situations, which led to improved customer satisfaction and a reduction in carrying costs.

Enhancing Visibility with Real-Time Tracking

A multinational manufacturing firm implemented real-time tracking of its shipments using IoT devices. This initiative provided end-to-end visibility into the supply chain, allowing the company to monitor the location and condition of goods in transit. The data collected enabled the firm to identify bottlenecks, reduce transit times, and respond proactively to potential disruptions, thus improving overall supply chain efficiency.

An automotive company developed a supplier performance scorecard system powered by analytics. By collecting and analyzing data on supplier delivery times, quality metrics, and compliance rates, the company was able to rank suppliers effectively. This led to more informed supplier selection, better negotiation leverage, and an overall increase in supply chain reliability and quality.

A logistics provider incorporated advanced analytics into its transportation management system to optimize delivery routes. The system considered factors such as traffic conditions, delivery windows, and vehicle capacity constraints. By implementing these optimized routes, the provider achieved significant reductions in fuel consumption, improved delivery times, and increased overall profitability.

A heavy machinery manufacturer applied prescriptive analytics to maximize the utilization of its manufacturing assets. The analytics platform recommended production schedules based on equipment maintenance cycles, workforce availability, and demand forecasts. This approach resulted in a substantial decrease in downtime, higher production output, and more efficient use of resources.

A consumer electronics company used sentiment analysis to gauge customer feedback on social media and online forums. This data informed the product development process, leading to design improvements that resonated with consumers. As a result, the company experienced an uptick in customer satisfaction ratings and saw a positive impact on sales.

A food and beverage company employed predictive modeling to refine its JIT inventory approach. By predicting peaks in demand with high accuracy, the company was able to synchronize its production and delivery schedules accordingly. This minimized inventory holding costs and ensured fresh products were available to customers, exemplifying the benefits of a lean supply chain.

A fashion retailer integrated analytics into its supply chain to identify waste reduction opportunities. By analyzing data on material usage, production inefficiencies, and customer purchasing patterns, the company made more sustainable choices in sourcing and production. This not only reduced waste but also enhanced the brand's image and appeal to eco-conscious consumers.

A telecommunications firm utilized market intelligence analytics to inform its sourcing strategies. By analyzing market trends, commodity prices, and supplier financial health, the company was able to make strategic purchasing decisions that mitigated risk and secured cost advantages.

Resilience Building through Predictive Risk Management

A pharmaceutical company leveraged predictive analytics to anticipate and manage supply chain risks. By modeling various risk scenarios, such as raw material shortages or geopolitical upheavals, the company developed contingency plans. This proactive risk management approach allowed the company to maintain continuity of supply, even in the face of unforeseen disruptions.

They demonstrate that when analytics are effectively integrated into supply chain operations, they can create significant value, enhance performance, and drive strategic outcomes. Through these real-world examples, we can derive best practices and lessons learned that can be applied across industries to achieve similar levels of success in the realm of supply chain analytics.

Integration of Supply Chain Analytics in Business Strategy

In the grand tapestry of business, supply chain analytics does not exist in isolation; it is a critical thread interwoven into the broader strategic fabric. The integration of supply chain analytics into business strategy is not merely a value-added option but a fundamental component of contemporary business practices.

For supply chain analytics to contribute meaningfully to business strategy, there must be a deliberate alignment with the organization's objectives. A company's strategic vision should guide the development and application of analytical tools and models, ensuring that the insights generated lead to actions that support the company's goals. Data-driven decision-making becomes the cornerstone of this alignment, relying on robust analytics to inform tactics and strategy.

Leveraging supply chain analytics can yield a competitive edge. By analyzing market trends, customer behavior, and operational efficiency, businesses can anticipate changes in the market and adapt swiftly, outpacing competitors. The strategic integration of analytics allows for a more proactive and pre-emptive business model, rather than a reactive one.

When supply chain analytics is integrated into business strategy, it necessitates cross-functional collaboration. Breaking down silos and fostering communication between departments ensure that insights are shared and acted upon holistically. Analytics thus becomes the language of collaboration, translating complex data into actionable intelligence across all levels of the organization.

Supply chain analytics, when strategically integrated, can become a driver of innovation. By analyzing and optimizing supply chain processes, companies can uncover opportunities for product enhancements, new business models, and service offerings. The supply chain is not just a cost center but a hub of innovation that can contribute significantly to the strategic growth of the business.

In a world where customer expectations are ever-evolving, analytics provide the means to develop customer-centric strategies. Understanding customer needs and preferences through data helps businesses tailor their offerings, optimize service levels, and ensure customer satisfaction. The integration of this understanding into the business strategy ensures that the supply chain is responsive to the market's demands.

Supply chain analytics plays a pivotal role in risk management and building strategic resilience. By analyzing historical and real-time data, businesses can identify risk patterns and develop strategies to mitigate them. This proactive approach to risk management ensures that the supply chain becomes a resilient asset, capable of withstanding and adapting to disruptions.

The strategic integration of supply chain analytics also extends to sustainability and ethical practices. Analytics can help businesses monitor and manage their environmental impact, optimize resource use, and ensure ethical labor practices across the supply chain. This not only aligns with regulatory and consumer demands but also positions the company as a socially responsible entity.

Supply chain analytics affords businesses the ability to customize and flex their strategies. By providing insights into various scenarios, analytics supports dynamic and flexible strategic execution, allowing businesses to pivot as needed in response to supply chain or market shifts.

Investment decisions and resource allocation are enhanced through the strategic use of supply chain analytics. By identifying areas of inefficiency and opportunity, businesses can make informed decisions about where to invest and how to allocate resources, ensuring that the supply chain is optimized and aligned with strategic objectives.

Finally, the integration of supply chain analytics into business strategy fosters a culture of continuous learning and evolution. As businesses implement analytical insights, they must also be prepared to learn from outcomes and evolve their strategies. This iterative process ensures that the supply chain remains agile and responsive to the changing business landscape.

In essence, the strategic integration of supply chain analytics is not just about data analysis; it is about embedding a data-centric mindset into the DNA of the organization. It is about leveraging insights to inform every strategic decision, ensuring that the supply chain is a robust engine driving the business forward. As companies navigate the complexities of the modern market, those who adeptly meld analytics with strategy will not only survive but thrive.

CHAPTER 2: DATA MANAGEMENT IN SUPPLY CHAIN ANALYTICS

Fundamentals of Data Management

D ata management serves as the backbone of supply chain analytics, providing the structural integrity required to handle vast quantities of information with agility and precision. At its core, data management encompasses the practices, architectural techniques, and tools designed to ensure that data is accurate, available, and secure across an organization. It is the meticulous orchestration of data acquisition, validation, storage, protection, and processing.

The journey of data management begins with the acquisition of high-quality data. In the realm of supply chains, data can emerge from a myriad of sources: transaction records, sensors, enterprise resource planning (ERP) systems, customer feedback, and beyond. It is paramount that each datum is rigorously validated for accuracy and completeness. Validation procedures, such as data profiling and cleansing, help ensure that the analysis is built on a solid foundation, free from the distortions of erroneous information.

Storage and Organization: The Pillars of Accessibility

Once acquired, data must be stored in a manner that balances accessibility with security. The choice between traditional data warehouses and modern data lakes, or a hybrid approach, often depends on the nature of the data and the analytical tools to be employed. Data organization, involving the classification and indexing of data, is critical to facilitate efficient retrieval and analysis. Proper organization allows for a streamlined flow of information, ensuring that relevant data points are readily available for analytical processes.

Protection: The Shield of Integrity

Data protection is not merely a regulatory compliance issue; it is a fundamental aspect of maintaining trust and integrity within the supply chain. Robust encryption, access controls, and consistent backups are essential to safeguard data against breaches and losses. In a digital ecosystem where threats are ever-present, a strong defense is as crucial as the insights the data promises to deliver.

Processing: The Engine of Transformation

Data processing encompasses the techniques and technologies employed to transform raw data into meaningful insights. Through processes such as Extract, Transform, Load (ETL), data is refined and prepared for analysis. Efficient data processing not only facilitates the seamless flow of information but also enables the application of complex analytical models that drive decision-making in supply chain management.

Governance: The Compass of Data Management

Data governance provides the strategic framework for data management, defining the policies, standards, and procedures that dictate how data is handled within an organization. Effective governance ensures consistency, reliability, and accountability in data management practices, aligning them with the broader objectives of supply chain analytics.

The interplay between data management and analytics is a symbiotic one. Without robust data management, analytics can be likened to a ship without a rudder—laden with potential but directionless. Conversely, data management without analytics is a treasure trove left unexplored. It is through the harmonization of these disciplines that supply chain analytics can yield transformative insights, driving efficiency, innovation, and competitive advantage.

Data management is not a static component of supply chain analytics; it is a dynamic enabler of strategy and performance. The principles of data management, when applied judiciously, empower organizations to harness the full spectrum of data's potential. As businesses continue to navigate the complexities of global supply chains, the role of data management will only grow in significance, underpinning the analytical capabilities that shape the future of supply chain excellence.

Importance of Data Quality and Governance

The intersection of data quality and governance forms a crucial nexus in supply chain analytics, where the caliber of insights is directly proportional to the integrity of the underlying data. This section expounds on the importance of maintaining high data quality and the role of governance in achieving this objective within the supply chain domain.

Data quality is paramount as it determines the reliability of analytics outputs. High-quality data is characterized by attributes such as accuracy, completeness, timeliness, consistency, and relevance. These attributes ensure that supply chain decisions are grounded in reality and reflective of current market dynamics. Inaccurate or outdated data can lead to costly errors, such as overstocking or underestimating demand, which can ripple through the supply chain and negatively impact customer satisfaction and profitability.

Accuracy and completeness form the bedrock of data quality. Accurate data reflects the true state of supply chain events and transactions, while completeness ensures that no critical elements are missing from the analysis. Both are indispensable for crafting a holistic view of the supply chain and for enabling precise decision-making.

In the fast-paced world of supply chains, timeliness of data is the pulse that drives responsiveness. The ability to act swiftly on current data can be the difference between capitalizing on a market opportunity and missing it entirely. Timely data empowers organizations to respond to changing conditions with agility, adjusting strategies to optimize performance and mitigate risks.

Consistency in data across various systems and departments ensures that everyone in the organization is working with the same set of facts. It eliminates discrepancies that could lead to conflicting analyses and misaligned strategies. Relevance, on the other hand, ensures that the data collected and analyzed is appropriate for the questions being asked and the decisions being made, akin to selecting the right instruments for a symphony to create harmony.

Data governance is the steering mechanism that guides the ship of data integrity through the tumultuous seas of supply chain operations. It involves the establishment of policies, roles, responsibilities, and processes that oversee the proper management of data assets. Governance ensures that data quality is not left to chance but is a deliberate outcome of stringent standards and controls.

Data governance fosters a culture of data stewardship where data is treated as a valuable corporate asset. Stewardship involves the careful management of data throughout its lifecycle, from creation to archiving, ensuring that it remains a reliable resource for analytics. This culture is essential in instilling the discipline required for maintaining data quality across the organization.

The impact of data quality on supply chain analytics is profound. Quality data is the fuel that powers sophisticated analytics engines, from predictive models to AI-driven simulations. Without it, even the most advanced analytical tools and methodologies cannot produce actionable insights. Therefore, investing in data quality and governance is not merely a best practice; it is a strategic imperative for any organization seeking to leverage analytics for supply chain optimization.

In summary, the importance of data quality and governance in supply chain analytics cannot be overstated. It is a continual pursuit of excellence that requires vigilance, commitment, and a proactive approach. Organizations that prioritize these aspects will find themselves well-equipped to navigate the complexities of the global supply chain, making informed decisions that drive success and sustainable growth.

Big Data in Supply Chain Analytics

In the realm of supply chain analytics, the advent of big data has been a game-changer, revolutionizing how organizations gather, analyze, and act on information. This section delves into the transformative impact of big data on the field, exploring its implications for enhancing efficiency, responsiveness, and strategic decision-making in supply chains.

Big data in supply chain refers to the vast quantities of structured and unstructured data generated from myriad sources such as sensors, social media, transaction records, and GPS signals. The challenge and opportunity lie in harnessing this torrent of data to extract meaningful insights that can deliver competitive advantage.

Structured data, typically stored in traditional databases, is readily searchable and organized in a defined manner, whereas unstructured data, such as text, images, and video, lacks a pre-defined data model, making it more complex to process and interpret. Big data analytics encompasses tools and techniques capable of handling both data types, thereby unlocking a more comprehensive understanding of supply chain operations.

The Four V's of Big Data: Volume, Velocity, Variety, Veracity

1. **Volume:** The sheer scale of data available can be overwhelming but also holds the key to uncovering patterns and trends that smaller datasets may not reveal.

2. **Velocity:** The speed at which new data is generated and flows into an organization dictates the need for real-time or near-real-time analytics to stay abreast of market conditions.

3. **Variety:** The diverse sources and types of data require robust analytics platforms that can integrate and interpret disparate data streams.

4. **Veracity:** The trustworthiness of data sources is critical, as the accuracy of insights depends on the quality of the data fed into analytic processes.

Big Data Analytics Techniques

Big data analytics employs a suite of sophisticated techniques to process and analyze large datasets. Machine learning algorithms, for instance, can identify patterns and predict outcomes, enabling supply chains to anticipate demand spikes or supply disruptions. Similarly, natural language processing (NLP) can sift through customer feedback on social media to gauge sentiment and inform customer relationship strategies.

Predictive analytics uses historical and real-time data to forecast future events, offering supply chains the foresight to preemptively manage risks and opportunities. Prescriptive analytics goes a step further, suggesting actions to take based on predictive insights, thus empowering supply chain managers to make informed decisions that align with business goals.

The integration of big data with the Internet of Things (IoT) has created a synergistic relationship where the constant stream of data from connected devices can be analyzed to monitor performance, predict maintenance needs, and optimize logistics routes. The result is a more responsive and agile supply chain that can adapt to dynamic market conditions.

The strategic value of big data in supply chain analytics is its ability to turn information into intelligence and intelligence into action. By leveraging big data, organizations can move beyond traditional reactive approaches and embrace proactive strategies that drive efficiency, cost savings, and customer satisfaction.

Despite the potential benefits, implementing big data analytics in supply chains is not without its challenges. It requires a robust IT infrastructure, skilled personnel, and a culture that values data-driven decision-making. Organizations must navigate these complexities with a clear strategy and an eye towards future scalability.

Big data has opened up new frontiers for supply chain analytics, providing deeper insights and enabling more sophisticated decision-making. As organizations continue to embrace big data, those who can effectively manage and analyze it will be well-positioned to lead the way in supply chain innovation and performance.

Data Warehousing and Data Lakes

In the ever-expanding digital landscape of supply chain management, data warehousing and data lakes represent critical repositories for storing and organizing the massive inflows of data. This section will elucidate the distinct roles and synergies between data warehouses and data lakes within the context of supply chain analytics, spotlighting their strategic importance in driving actionable insights.

A data warehouse is a centralized repository tailored for query and analysis. It is structured to provide a uniform format for different data types, which is crucial for comparative analysis and reporting. In supply chain analytics, data warehousing facilitates the consolidation of data from various sources, including inventory levels, supplier performance, and customer orders, enabling a cohesive view of operations.

The architecture of a data warehouse is typically composed of tiers: the database server where data is stored, the analytics engine that processes queries, and the front-end client that presents data in an intelligible format for decision-makers. This architecture supports the Extract, Transform, Load (ETL) process, which is pivotal in cleaning, integrating, and refreshing data to ensure its relevance and accuracy.

Contrastingly, a data lake is a vast pool of raw data, the majority of which is held in its native format until it is needed. Data lakes accommodate the high-velocity, high-variety, and high-volume attributes of big data, allowing for the storage of unstructured data such as machine logs, sensor data, and images that cannot be neatly fitted into the rows and columns of traditional databases.

The flexibility of a data lake lies in its ability to grow with the needs of the business, offering a scalable solution that can accommodate the exponential growth of data without the need for extensive pre-processing. This adaptability makes data lakes an attractive option for companies grappling with the complexities of managing big data.

A hybrid approach, leveraging both data warehousing and data lakes, is often the most effective strategy for supply chain analytics. This approach harnesses the structured analytical power of data warehouses for operational reporting and the unstructured, exploratory capabilities of data lakes for advanced analytics pursuits, such as predictive modeling and machine learning.

The interplay between data warehouses and data lakes becomes particularly potent when combined with big data analytics. Data warehouses can feed curated, structured data into analytic models, while data lakes can be mined for insights using advanced analytic tools capable of handling unstructured data, thereby offering a comprehensive analytical framework.

Effective data governance is paramount when managing both data warehouses and data lakes. It ensures that the data within these repositories remains accurate, consistent, and secure. Maintaining high data quality is essential, as the outputs of analytic processes are only as good as the data inputs.

The strategic imperative of implementing data warehousing and data lakes lies in their capacity to provide a nuanced, multi-layered view of the supply chain. They serve as the bedrock upon which sophisticated analytics are performed, transforming raw data into strategic insights that can lead to optimized supply chain performance.

Data warehousing and data lakes are the analytic powerhouses of supply chain analytics. They each serve unique, complementary roles in the storage, management, and analysis of data. By strategically utilizing both, organizations can ensure that they are equipped to handle the complexities of modern supply chain data and derive meaningful insights that drive competitive advantage.

Technologies for Managing and Processing Data

Emerging from the depths of data warehousing and lakes, we venture into the dynamic world of technologies that are instrumental in managing and processing this data. This segment delves into the innovative tools and systems that bolster the capabilities of supply chain managers to harness the full potential of their data assets.

In the realm of supply chain analytics, the profusion of data management technologies has catalyzed a revolution in how data is manipulated to yield insights. These technologies range from traditional database management systems to cutting-edge software that specializes in big data processing.

A DBMS serves as the backbone of data management, providing a structured environment for data storage, retrieval, and management. Its functions are critical in maintaining the integrity of data within both warehouses and lakes. It ensures that data is accessible, consistent, and efficiently managed throughout its lifecycle.

Advanced analytics platforms step in to handle complex data analyses that go beyond the capabilities of a traditional DBMS. These platforms integrate with existing data repositories and use sophisticated algorithms to perform tasks such as predictive analytics, data mining, and machine learning.

In-memory computing accelerates the processing of large volumes of data by storing it in RAM instead of on hard disks, offering near real-time analytics. This technology is particularly useful in supply chain applications where speed is of the essence, such as in demand forecasting and real-time inventory management.

For data that arrives in a continuous stream, such as IoT sensor data, stream processing software is indispensable. It allows for the analysis of data in motion, providing the ability to make decisions on-the-fly and respond to supply chain events as they occur.

Data virtualization presents a way to manage and access data across multiple sources without the need to physically consolidate it. It offers a unified view of data scattered across various systems, enhancing the agility of decision-making processes in the supply chain.

ETL tools are vital for the transformation and integration of data from disparate sources into a data warehouse. They automate the process of extracting data, transforming it into a consistent format, and loading it into a central repository, ensuring that data is accurate and up-to-date.

Ensuring the quality of data is non-negotiable in supply chain analytics. Data quality management software assists in cleaning, de-duplicating, and validating data to maintain its integrity. This software is crucial in preventing the propagation of errors that could lead to costly misjudgments.

The cloud has emerged as a powerhouse for data management, offering scalable and cost-effective solutions. Cloud-based platforms provide on-demand access to a suite of tools for data storage, processing, and analytics, along with the benefits of enhanced security and disaster recovery options.

AI and machine learning technologies are increasingly interwoven with data management tools, automating complex processes and uncovering patterns that would be imperceptible to the human eye. Their role is expanding in supply chain analytics, from optimizing routing algorithms to predicting maintenance needs.

While the array of technologies for managing and processing data is ever-growing, the challenge lies in their integration. It is essential to create a seamless ecosystem where data flows unimpeded between systems, and technologies complement each other to provide a holistic view of the supply chain.

The array of technologies for managing and processing data are the enablers of analytical excellence. They provide the mechanisms through which vast and varied data can be transformed into actionable intelligence. In the context of supply chain analytics, these technologies are not just tools but strategic assets that empower organizations to navigate the complexities of modern supply chains with agility and insight.

Data Integration and ETL Processes

Navigating the intricate web of data integration, we encounter the cornerstone of any robust analytics framework: the ETL processes. Extract, Transform, Load (ETL) is the triad that orchestrates the harmonious movement of data from its source to a centralized repository.

The ETL process can be likened to a symphony, where each movement is a meticulous operation that transforms raw data into a refined asset, ready for analysis.

The extraction phase initiates the process, involving the careful retrieval of data from numerous sources. This can include databases, CRM systems, ERP systems, and various other repositories, both structured and unstructured. The goal here is to gather the necessary data without compromising its original state.

Transformation is the crescendo of the ETL process, where data undergoes cleansing, de-duplication, normalization, and enrichment. It is in this stage that disparate data is harmonized, errors are rectified, and data is sculpted into a format that's analytically viable. Transformations can range from simple calculations to complex business logic applications.

The finale of the ETL process is the loading phase, where the data is carefully deposited into the target data warehouse or data lake. It is crucial that this step is performed with precision to ensure data integrity and availability.

Best Practices in ETL

- Incremental loading, which minimizes the load on operational systems and allows for more frequent updates.

- Ensuring idempotence, where re-running ETL processes does not result in duplicate entries.

- Data profiling and quality checks at every stage to preemptively address data anomalies.

The evolution of data integration has given rise to variations such as ELT (Extract, Load, Transform), where transformation occurs after loading into the target system, leveraging the computational power of modern data warehouses. Additionally, data pipelines have emerged, offering a more continuous and automated flow of data, suitable for real-time analytics.

ETL processes also play a pivotal role in data governance. They enforce rules and policies that ensure data quality and compliance with regulatory standards. The lineage of data —its origin, journey, and transformations—is meticulously documented, providing auditable trails that are essential for governance.

A plethora of ETL tools exist, ranging from commercial solutions like Informatica and Talend to open-source options such as Apache NiFi and Airflow. The choice of tool is often dictated by factors such as the volume of data, variety of data sources, complexity of transformations, and the organization's technical maturity.

ETL processes are increasingly integrating with advanced analytics to enable more sophisticated data manipulation. This includes the use of machine learning algorithms to predict and rectify data quality issues, and natural language processing to interpret and categorize unstructured data.

ETL is both an art and a science, necessitating a blend of technical acumen and strategic foresight. It is the foundation upon which reliable, timely, and actionable insights are built. In the context of supply chain analytics, ETL is not just about moving data; it's about crafting a data ecosystem that is robust, compliant, and primed for discovery. As we progress through the narrative of this book, the importance of ETL in the larger analytics machinery will continue to be a recurrent theme, one that underscores the transformative power of data in driving supply chain excellence.

Data Security and Privacy Considerations

In the digital age, where data is as valuable as currency, the sanctity of data security and privacy becomes paramount. As we delve into this realm, we acknowledge the dual responsibility of protecting sensitive information and respecting individual privacy rights within the context of supply chain analytics.

Data security is the vanguard that shields the troves of sensitive supply chain data from unauthorized access and cyber threats. It encompasses a suite of practices and protocols designed to defend against breaches that could lead to data corruption or theft.

Encryption stands as a primary defense mechanism, converting data into a coded format that is impervious to intruders without the correct decryption key. Employing robust encryption standards for data at rest and in transit ensures that even if a breach occurs, the information remains unintelligible and secure.

Implementing stringent access controls is akin to appointing a vigilant gatekeeper. It ensures that only authorized individuals have the ability to interact with data. This includes the application of the principle of least privilege, where users are granted the minimum level of access necessary to perform their duties.

Maintaining comprehensive audit trails is essential for monitoring who accessed what data and when. This chronicling of data interactions serves as a deterrent to malicious activities and is crucial for forensic analysis in the aftermath of a security incident.

Privacy considerations are not merely ethical obligations but also legal mandates. Regulations such as the General Data Protection Regulation (GDPR) and the California Consumer Privacy Act (CCPA) prescribe stringent guidelines for data handling and grant individuals unprecedented control over their personal information.

Anonymization and pseudonymization are techniques used to obscure or remove identifying information from data sets. This ensures that individuals' privacy is maintained while still allowing for the aggregate analysis crucial for supply chain improvements.

No fortress is impregnable. In the event of a data breach, having a robust incident response plan is critical. This includes immediate steps to contain the breach, notification procedures to alert affected parties, and post-mortem analysis to prevent future occurrences.

The supply chain is only as strong as its weakest link. Managing risks associated with vendors and third parties involves conducting regular security assessments and ensuring that partners adhere to the same data protection standards.

The goal within supply chain analytics is to harness the power of data while upholding security and privacy. This balance is achieved through techniques such as data masking and differential privacy, which allow for the utilization of data insights without exposing sensitive details.

Lastly, it is imperative to recognize that technology alone cannot safeguard data. Educating employees about security best practices and fostering a culture of privacy are equally vital. This human element is often the first line of defense against phishing attacks and social engineering tactics.

Data security and privacy are not just operational considerations but deeply ethical ones. They reflect an organization's values and commitment to responsible stewardship of information. As we proceed to unravel the complexities of supply chain analytics, the need to integrate robust security and privacy measures into every facet of data management remains a theme interwoven throughout our discussions. It stands as a testament to the ethical imperative of protecting what has been entrusted to us by customers, suppliers, and employees alike.

Master Data Management (MDM)

Master Data Management, or MDM, emerges as the backbone of data integrity within the supply chain. It is the foundational process that defines, stores, and maintains the core business entities of an organization with the highest level of consistency and quality.

At the heart of MDM lie several key pillars designed to uphold the accuracy and uniformity of master data across the enterprise.

Establishing a central repository for master data is akin to creating a 'single source of truth'. This repository becomes the authoritative reference for all critical business entities, including products, customers, suppliers, and assets.

Data stewards are the custodians charged with the maintenance and governance of master data. Their role is pivotal in ensuring that the data adheres to defined standards and remains accurate throughout its lifecycle.

Data governance provides the framework for data management policies and procedures. It ensures compliance with internal and external regulations and fosters alignment between MDM efforts and business objectives.

Standardization involves the creation of uniform data formats, while harmonization aligns disparate data across different systems. Together, they form the common language that facilitates seamless communication within and across organizational boundaries.

The pursuit of high data quality is relentless in MDM. It involves ongoing efforts to cleanse, de-duplicate, and enrich data, setting the benchmark for excellence that supports informed decision-making.

Integration is the art of seamlessly connecting the central repository with various business applications and systems. It ensures that master data flows appropriately throughout the organization, supporting operational processes and analytics.

MDM also manages the hierarchies and relationships between master data entities. This organizational map provides context and structure, enabling complex analyses such as network optimization and spend analysis.

In the realm of supply chain analytics, MDM plays an instrumental role.

Clean, consistent master data is the fuel that powers advanced analytics engines. It ensures that predictive models and algorithms generate accurate insights for strategic decision-making.

MDM supports the personalization of customer experiences by providing a holistic view of customer data. This enables tailored marketing campaigns and product recommendations that resonate with individual preferences.

Accurate supplier data enhances collaboration and negotiation. It allows for the segmentation of suppliers based on performance, risk profile, and strategic importance, leading to more effective supplier engagement.

Regulatory compliance hinges on the traceability and integrity of master data. MDM helps in adhering to standards such as ISO certifications and industry-specific regulations, mitigating the risk of non-compliance.

Master Data Management is not merely a technical initiative but a strategic asset that can unlock the full potential of supply chain operations and analytics. It demands a concerted effort across the organization to build a robust MDM framework. As we progress further, the significance of MDM in supporting the analytical capabilities necessary for competing in today's complex supply chain environment becomes increasingly evident. The sophistication it brings to the fore is pivotal in achieving the precision and agility required to thrive in the ever-evolving landscape of global commerce.

Collaborative Data Management across the Supply Chain

In the intricate web of supply chain operations, collaborative data management becomes the linchpin for synchronicity and efficiency. It is the rigorous practice of sharing, managing, and utilizing data across all entities involved in the supply chain to achieve a harmonious operational ecosystem.

The essence of collaboration in data management is to synchronize efforts towards a unified objective. Just as an orchestra's sections must be in harmony to create a symphony, every participant in the supply chain must align their data to ensure a seamless flow of goods and information.

The creation of exchange platforms is essential for collaborative data management. These digital arenas enable the secure transfer of real-time data between suppliers, manufacturers, distributors, and retailers, ensuring that all parties have access to the necessary information to make informed decisions.

Interoperability is the ability of different information systems and software applications to communicate effectively. It is vital for collaborative data management as it breaks down the silos that hinder the free flow of information.

Transparency in the supply chain is achieved through collaborative data management. By granting visibility into operations, inventory levels, and demand forecasts, it builds trust among partners and allows for better coordination and planning.

Developing a shared language through standard data formats and protocols is crucial. This standardization simplifies the exchange of information and reduces the risk of misinterpretation, which can lead to costly errors.

When data is managed collaboratively, it can be pooled to perform collective analytics. This approach enables benchmarking against industry standards and derives insights that benefit all parties, leading to a more competitive and agile supply chain.

Emerging technologies such as blockchain and cloud-based platforms are catalysts for collaborative data management. They provide secure, scalable, and accessible means for sharing data, ensuring integrity and non-repudiation in transactions.

A supply chain that effectively manages data in a collaborative manner can respond more swiftly to customer needs. The integration of customer feedback and demand signals across the supply chain allows for proactive adjustments and enhances the overall customer experience.

Despite its benefits, collaborative data management is not without challenges. Issues such as data privacy concerns, disparate IT systems, and resistance to change can impede the implementation of a collaborative approach.

To overcome these hurdles, establishing strategic partnerships and alliances is essential. By fostering a culture of open communication and mutual benefit, supply chain entities can navigate the complexities of collaborative data management.

Collaborative data management is a catalyst for innovation in the supply chain. It encourages a holistic approach to problem-solving, where shared challenges are met with unified solutions. It is this collaborative spirit, underpinned by robust data management practices, that will pave the way for supply chains that are not only efficient and resilient but also adaptive and forward-looking in the face of global market shifts and technological advancements.

Cloud Computing and Its Impact on Data Management

Cloud computing has revolutionized the way data is managed within the supply chain, ushering in an era of unprecedented agility and scalability. The paradigm shift from traditional on-premises storage and processing to cloud-based services has profound implications for data management, affecting everything from accessibility to cost-efficiency.

Cloud services offer a level of scalability that is simply unattainable with conventional IT infrastructure. Supply chains can now adjust their data storage and computational resources with ease, scaling up or down as demand fluctuates. This flexibility is critical in managing the ebb and flow of supply chain activities and in accommodating business growth without the need for significant capital expenditure.

The financial model of cloud computing, typically based on pay-per-use, presents an attractive proposition for supply chains. It transforms data management from a capital-intensive operation to an operational expense, freeing up capital for other strategic investments.

One of the most significant advantages of cloud computing is the ability to access data from anywhere at any time. This accessibility empowers supply chain stakeholders to make informed decisions on the go, fostering a more responsive and dynamic operational framework.

Cloud platforms facilitate a new level of cooperation among supply chain partners. With shared access to cloud-based applications and databases, stakeholders can work on common datasets in real-time, streamlining processes and enhancing communication.

While the cloud offers many benefits, it also brings challenges in terms of security and compliance. Protecting sensitive supply chain data in a cloud environment requires robust security protocols and adherence to regulatory standards. Cloud service providers typically invest heavily in security, offering a level of protection that may be difficult for individual companies to achieve independently.

The integrative nature of cloud services allows for seamless connections between disparate systems, providing a cohesive view of the supply chain. This interoperability is crucial for end-to-end visibility and informed decision-making.

Cloud computing provides robust disaster recovery and business continuity solutions. Data backups and recovery processes are managed by the cloud service provider, ensuring that supply chain operations can continue with minimal disruption in the event of a disaster.

The power of cloud computing extends to advanced data analytics. Cloud-based analytics tools can process large volumes of data quickly, providing actionable insights that drive strategic supply chain decisions.

The cloud's shared resource model promotes a more sustainable approach to IT. By utilizing centralized data centers that optimize energy consumption, supply chains can reduce their carbon footprint, contributing to environmental sustainability goals.

As the supply chain landscape becomes increasingly complex, cloud computing stands as a beacon of innovation and efficiency. Preparing for a cloud-driven future involves strategic planning, investment in the right technologies, and a commitment to upskilling the workforce to harness the full potential of cloud-based data management.

The integration of cloud computing into supply chain analytics signifies a leap towards a more interconnected, intelligent, and resilient supply chain ecosystem. It is through the adoption of such transformative technologies that supply chains can not only adapt to the demands of an ever-changing market landscape but also anticipate and shape future trends.

CHAPTER 3: DEMAND FORECASTING AND PLANNING

Role of Demand Forecasting in Supply Chain

D emand forecasting serves as the cornerstone of effective supply chain management, balancing the scales between supply and demand in an ever-shifting marketplace. It is a predictive process that leverages historical data, market analysis, and statistical algorithms to anticipate customer demand. This foresight enables businesses to make strategic decisions that minimize waste, optimize inventory levels, and ensure customer satisfaction.

At the heart of demand forecasting lies the ability to align supply chain operations with business strategy. By predicting future demand with a reasonable degree of accuracy, companies can tailor their production schedules, workforce allocation, and inventory levels accordingly. This alignment ensures that resources are utilized efficiently, reducing costs and enhancing the company's ability to respond swiftly to market changes.

Effective demand forecasting is critical to maintaining optimal inventory levels. Overestimating demand can lead to excess inventory, increased holding costs, and potential obsolescence, while underestimating can result in stockouts, lost sales, and customer dissatisfaction. Forecasting provides the insights necessary to strike the right balance, ensuring that inventory levels are congruent with actual market demand.

The ripple effects of accurate forecasting extend throughout the supply chain, from procurement to distribution. Suppliers can be notified in advance of expected order volumes, allowing for better coordination and planning. This proactive approach helps to avoid bottlenecks and ensures a smoother flow of materials and products through the supply chain.

Demand forecasting is not merely about having the right products in stock; it's also about delivering exceptional service. By understanding demand patterns, companies can optimize service levels, ensuring that customers receive their products in a timely and reliable manner. This reliability builds trust and loyalty, which are essential in today's competitive marketplace.

While forecasting is inherently uncertain due to the dynamic nature of markets, it still plays a crucial role in risk management. Forecasts act as an early warning system, allowing businesses to identify potential demand shifts and develop contingency plans. This proactive stance mitigates risk and provides a framework for dealing with uncertainty.

Advancements in technology, particularly in the realms of machine learning and artificial intelligence, have significantly enhanced the accuracy of demand forecasting. Algorithms can now detect patterns and trends in large datasets that may be imperceptible to the human eye, leading to more precise forecasts. These technological tools also enable real-time data analysis, allowing for forecasts to be updated continuously as new information becomes available.

Consider a global electronics manufacturer that implemented a state-of-the-art demand forecasting system. By analyzing sales data, market trends, and consumer behavior, the company was able to predict product demand with a high degree of accuracy. This led to a 20% reduction in inventory holding costs and a 15% increase in customer service levels, illustrating the profound impact that effective demand forecasting can have on the bottom line.

In essence, demand forecasting is the art and science of predicting the future in a way that brings tangible benefits to the present. It is a critical function that enables supply chains to be agile, adaptive, and customer-centric. As businesses continue to navigate the complexities of global markets, the role of demand forecasting becomes ever more pivotal in achieving operational excellence and strategic success.

Statistical Forecasting Models

Statistical forecasting models are the engines that drive the predictive power of demand forecasting. They process historical data to identify patterns and relationships that can be used to project future trends. The choice of the right statistical model is crucial, as it directly impacts the accuracy of the forecast.

Quantitative forecasting models: rely on numerical data to forecast future demand. These models fall into two primary categories: time series models and causal models. Time series models, such as moving averages, exponential smoothing, and autoregressive integrated moving average (ARIMA), focus on patterns found in historical data over time. Causal models, like regression analysis, examine the relationship between demand and other variables, such as price or economic indicators.

The moving average model: is one of the simplest statistical forecasting methods. It calculates the average demand over a specific number of past periods, smoothing out short-term fluctuations. This model is particularly effective in stable environments with minimal trend or seasonal variations. However, its simplicity can also be a limitation, as it may not respond quickly to sudden changes in demand patterns.

Exponential smoothing models: are a step up in complexity from moving averages. They assign exponentially decreasing weights to past observations, giving more importance to recent data. This approach makes the model more responsive to trends and seasonal effects. The Holt-Winters method is an extension of exponential smoothing that can handle data with both trend and seasonality.

ARIMA models: are sophisticated and versatile, suitable for a wide range of time series data. They can account for trends, seasonal patterns, and autocorrelation within the data. ARIMA models require careful parameter selection, which can be a complex process but, when done correctly, can yield highly accurate forecasts.

Regression analysis: is used to forecast demand based on the relationship between the dependent variable (demand) and one or more independent variables. This model can incorporate a variety of factors, such as marketing spend, economic conditions, or competitor actions, to predict how they will influence demand.

Choosing the Right Model: A Data-Driven Decision

1. The nature of the demand pattern (stable, trending, seasonal)

2. The availability and quality of historical data

3. The presence of causal relationships

4. The desired forecast horizon (short-term, medium-term, long-term)

Python Code Example: Implementing a Time Series Model

```python
import numpy as np
import pandas as pd
import statsmodels.api as sm

# Load historical demand data into a Pandas DataFrame
data = pd.read_csv('historical_demand.csv', index_col='date', parse_dates=True)

# Fit an exponential smoothing model
model = sm.tsa.ExponentialSmoothing(data['demand'], trend='add', seasonal='add', seasonal_periods=12).fit()

# Forecast the next 12 months of demand
forecast = model.forecast(12)

print(forecast)
```

` ` `

This example showcases the ease with which complex statistical models can be implemented and utilized to make informed decisions in a supply chain context.

Statistical forecasting models are indispensable tools for planning and decision-making in supply chains. They provide a structured approach to distilling insights from data, allowing businesses to anticipate future demand with greater precision. As technology advances and more data becomes available, the sophistication and accuracy of these models will continue to grow, offering supply chain professionals new opportunities to optimize their operations and stay ahead in a competitive landscape.

Machine Learning and AI in Forecasting

In the ever-evolving landscape of supply chain analytics, machine learning and artificial intelligence (AI) have emerged as transformative forces. These advanced technologies augment statistical models, providing a new dimension to demand forecasting by uncovering complex patterns and relationships that traditional methods may overlook.

Machine learning algorithms thrive on large datasets, finding hidden structures within them. Unlike traditional statistical models, these algorithms can automatically adapt to changes in demand patterns, making them highly effective for forecasting in volatile and complex market conditions. Machine learning models such as decision trees, random forests, and neural networks can handle non-linear relationships and interactions among multiple variables, leading to a nuanced understanding of demand drivers.

Neural networks, inspired by the human brain's architecture, are particularly potent for forecasting tasks. Their ability to learn from vast amounts of data and identify subtle patterns makes them well-suited for supply chain applications where numerous factors influence demand. Recurrent neural networks (RNNs) and Long Short-Term Memory networks (LSTMs) are especially adept at processing sequential data, capturing temporal dependencies essential for accurate time-series forecasting.

Ensemble techniques like boosting and bagging improve prediction accuracy by combining the outputs of multiple models. These methods can fine-tune forecasts by balancing the strengths and weaknesses of individual models, leading to a robust composite model that is less prone to overfitting and better at generalizing to unseen data.

AI in forecasting goes beyond mere prediction; it involves the use of advanced algorithms to automate and optimize decision-making processes. AI systems can continuously learn and adapt, incorporating real-time data feeds to update forecasts on the fly. This ability to dynamically adjust to new information enables supply chains to respond swiftly to market shifts, reducing lag time and improving responsiveness.

Python Code Example: Building a Neural Network with Keras

```python
from keras.models import Sequential
from keras.layers import Dense, LSTM
from sklearn.preprocessing import MinMaxScaler
import pandas as pd
```

```
# Load and preprocess the data
data = pd.read_csv('demand_data.csv')
scaler = MinMaxScaler(feature_range=(0, 1))
scaled_data = scaler.fit_transform(data.values)

# Define the neural network model
model = Sequential()
model.add(LSTM(units=50,                 return_sequences=True,
input_shape=(scaled_data.shape[1], 1)))
model.add(LSTM(units=50))
model.add(Dense(1))

# Compile and fit the model to the data
model.compile(optimizer='adam', loss='mean_squared_error')
model.fit(scaled_data, epochs=100, batch_size=32)

# Predict future demand
predicted_demand = model.predict(scaled_data)
```
` ` `

This example provides a glimpse into the implementation of AI in demand forecasting, showcasing the potential of neural networks to enhance predictive performance.

The Future Is Intelligent: Embracing AI

The integration of machine learning and AI into forecasting represents the vanguard of supply chain analytics. These technologies enable businesses to harness the power of their data like never before, turning it into actionable insights that drive strategic decisions. As machine learning and AI continue to advance, their impact on supply chain forecasting will only deepen, propelling organizations towards a future where agility and intelligence define their success.

In the next section, we will explore the collaborative approach of planning, forecasting, and replenishment, and how it intertwines with the technological advancements discussed thus far to create a synergistic effect in supply chain management.

Collaborative Planning, Forecasting, and Replenishment (CPFR)

Collaborative Planning, Forecasting, and Replenishment (CPFR) represents a significant leap in supply chain management, embodying a collective strategy where partners in a supply chain agree to work together using shared information and aligned processes to forecast demand. This system is built on trust, cooperation, and shared objectives, aiming to reduce inefficiencies and enhance the responsiveness of the supply chain to market demands.

At the heart of CPFR lies a framework that encourages the synchronization of production and distribution plans with actual consumer demand. This collaborative approach consists of several steps, starting with an agreement between partners to engage in the CPFR process. It proceeds through joint business planning, demand and supply management, execution, and analysis, all set against a backdrop of shared information.

The CPFR journey begins with partners developing a single, joint business plan that stipulates policies, procedures, and the shared metrics for monitoring performance. This plan lays the groundwork for a harmonious relationship where each party's capabilities and expectations are transparent and aligned.

Forecasting plays a pivotal role in CPFR, as partners share data and insights to create a single, accurate forecast that drives the planning of production and purchasing. By leveraging the predictive prowess of AI and machine learning models in the earlier phase, partners can integrate real-time market data and advanced analytics into their collaborative forecasts, resulting in a more precise and adaptable demand plan.

With a shared forecast in hand, partners execute the agreed-upon business plan, orchestrating production schedules, inventory deployment, and shipping in a coordinated effort to meet consumer demand efficiently. The integration of CPFR with execution systems, such as Enterprise Resource Planning (ERP) and Advanced Planning and Scheduling (APS) systems, ensures that decisions are informed by the most current and comprehensive view of the supply chain.

The final step in the CPFR model is the analysis phase, where partners review outcomes against their forecast and business plan. Here, they employ advanced analytics to identify variances, understand causes, and adapt strategies accordingly. Machine learning algorithms assist by recognizing patterns in the discrepancies and recommending corrective actions, facilitating a proactive approach to continuous improvement.

Python Code Example: Collaborative Forecasting with Scikit-Learn

```python
```

```
from sklearn.ensemble import RandomForestRegressor
from sklearn.metrics import mean_absolute_error
import pandas as pd

# Load and preprocess partner data
partner_data = pd.read_csv('partner_forecast_data.csv')
historical_sales = pd.read_csv('historical_sales_data.csv')

# Train the random forest model on historical data
rf_model     =     RandomForestRegressor(n_estimators=100,
random_state=42)
rf_model.fit(historical_sales.drop('Sales',          axis=1),
historical_sales['Sales'])

# Predict future sales using partner data
partner_forecasts = rf_model.predict(partner_data)

# Evaluate the forecast accuracy
mae      =        mean_absolute_error(historical_sales['Sales'],
partner_forecasts)
print(f"Mean Absolute Error: {mae}")
` ` `
```

This code snippet illustrates how partners can use machine learning to improve their collaborative forecasting efforts, harnessing the power of shared data to predict sales more accurately.

The convergence of CPFR and AI-driven forecasting methodologies is a testament to the evolution of supply chain management. By leveraging the strengths of collaboration and cutting-edge technologies, organizations can achieve a level of precision and efficiency previously unattainable. As these practices become increasingly integrated, the supply chain transforms into a responsive, anticipatory, and resilient network that not only meets but anticipates the needs of the modern market.

Moving forward, the book will address the impact of market dynamics on demand forecasting, further weaving the narrative of how external factors and internal strategies coalesce to sculpt the supply chain landscape.

Impact of Market Dynamics on Demand Forecasting

Understanding the impact of market dynamics on demand forecasting is akin to navigating a vessel through the ever-changing waters of the global marketplace.

underscores the importance of agility and adaptability in forecasting methodologies to account for the fluidity of market conditions.

Market dynamics are the patterns and changes in consumer behavior and market conditions that influence the demand for products and services. These dynamics can include economic indicators, consumer trends, seasonality, competitive actions, and technological advancements. Each of these factors can cause fluctuations in demand, and understanding their interplay is crucial for creating accurate demand forecasts.

Economic indicators, such as GDP growth, unemployment rates, and consumer confidence indexes, provide valuable insights into the health of the economy and consumer spending patterns. For instance, a rise in consumer confidence may signal an upcoming increase in discretionary spending, which in turn could affect demand for certain categories of products.

Trends in consumer behavior, such as preferences for sustainable products or the adoption of digital services, can drastically alter demand patterns. Forecasters must stay attuned to these trends and rapidly incorporate them into demand models to prevent stockouts or overstocking, which could result in lost sales or increased holding costs.

While some seasonal patterns are predictable, such as increased demand for certain products during holiday periods, unexpected events like unseasonal weather can disrupt these patterns. Advanced forecasting models that incorporate weather data and historical sales can help anticipate and respond to such anomalies.

Competitive actions, such as price changes, promotions, and new product launches, can have immediate and significant impacts on demand. By monitoring competitors and incorporating scenarios into forecasting models, companies can prepare for and react to these market shifts.

The rapid pace of technological change can both disrupt existing demand patterns and create new opportunities. Forecasters need to consider how emerging technologies might impact the market and adjust their demand forecasts to reflect these potential shifts.

To accurately forecast demand in the face of these complex market dynamics, companies must utilize sophisticated analytical tools that can digest large volumes of data and identify correlations and causal relationships. Machine learning models are particularly adept at this, as they can learn from historical data and adapt to new patterns as they emerge.

Python Code Example: Incorporating Economic Indicators into Forecasting

```python
import pandas as pd
from statsmodels.tsa.arima_model import ARIMA

# Load economic indicators and sales data
economic_data = pd.read_csv('economic_indicators.csv')
sales_data = pd.read_csv('product_sales_data.csv')

# Combine datasets based on the date
combined_data = pd.merge(sales_data, economic_data, on='Date')

# Create an ARIMA model to forecast sales with economic indicators
arima_model = ARIMA(combined_data['Sales'], order=(1, 1, 1), exog=combined_data.drop(['Sales', 'Date'], axis=1))
arima_results = arima_model.fit()

# Forecast future sales
forecast = arima_results.forecast(steps=5, exog=combined_data.drop(['Sales', 'Date'], axis=1).iloc[-5:])
print(f"Forecasted Sales: {forecast}")
```

In this code, economic indicators are used as exogenous variables in an ARIMA model to provide additional context for the sales forecast. This allows for a more nuanced forecast that takes into account the broader economic environment.

As market dynamics continue to evolve, so too must the strategies and tools used for demand forecasting. By embracing a flexible and responsive approach to forecasting, companies can better navigate the complexities of the marketplace and position themselves to meet consumer demand effectively and efficiently.

Demand Sensing and Shaping Strategies

Venturing beyond the realm of traditional forecasting, this section delves into the progressive domains of demand sensing and shaping strategies. By harnessing the power of real-time data and advanced analytics, businesses can fine-tune their demand predictions and even influence demand patterns in their favor, marking a significant evolution from passive forecasting to active demand management.

Demand sensing is a sophisticated approach that leverages near-term data to improve the accuracy of demand forecasts. It captures the pulse of current market conditions by analyzing real-time data streams from point-of-sale systems, social media, web traffic, and weather forecasts.

Real-time data offers a snapshot of current market conditions, allowing businesses to adjust their forecasts in response to immediate changes. For instance, sudden social media trends can lead to a spike in demand for specific products, and demand sensing can help companies anticipate and respond to these shifts more swiftly.

Machine learning algorithms play a pivotal role in demand

sensing. They can process vast amounts of diverse data and identify subtle patterns that might elude traditional forecasting methods. By continually learning from data, these algorithms become increasingly adept at predicting short-term demand fluctuations.

Python Code Example: Demand Sensing with Machine Learning

```python
import pandas as pd
from sklearn.ensemble import RandomForestRegressor

# Load real-time sales and external data
real_time_data = pd.read_csv('real_time_sales.csv')
external_data = pd.read_csv('external_data_sources.csv')

# Merge datasets to create a unified view
full_data = pd.merge(real_time_data, external_data, on='Timestamp')

# Prepare features and target variable
X = full_data.drop(['Sales', 'Timestamp'], axis=1)
y = full_data['Sales']

# Train a random forest regressor for demand sensing
rf_model = RandomForestRegressor(n_estimators=100, random_state=42)
rf_model.fit(X, y)
```

```
# Predict near-term demand
predicted_demand = rf_model.predict(X)
print(f"Predicted Demand: {predicted_demand}")
```
```

In this example, a Random Forest model is trained on real-time sales data combined with external data sources to predict near-term demand. The model can be updated frequently to reflect the latest market conditions.

Demand shaping involves strategic actions taken to influence the demand curve. It is a proactive stance where businesses actively manage demand through pricing strategies, promotions, product bundling, and targeted marketing campaigns.

Promotions and pricing strategies can be tailored to drive demand for overstocked items or to capitalize on emerging market trends. By adjusting these levers, businesses can smooth out demand variability and align supply with market demand.

Bundling products together or using cross-selling techniques can stimulate demand for items that complement best-sellers or new launches. These strategies can be tailored based on insights derived from customer behavior analytics.

Personalized marketing campaigns that resonate with specific customer segments can shape demand patterns. Leveraging customer data for personalization ensures that marketing efforts are more likely to result in increased sales.

Demand sensing and shaping are complementary strategies.
```

While sensing is about reacting to the market, shaping is about proactively influencing it. Together, they enable a dynamic approach to demand management that can significantly enhance supply chain responsiveness and efficiency.

As we forge ahead into the intricate tapestry of supply chain management, the combined use of demand sensing and shaping emerges as a beacon of innovation. By embracing these strategies, businesses can achieve a competitive edge, responding with agility to the ebb and flow of market demand.

The following section will introduce the concept of Sales and Operations Planning (S&OP), a critical process that harmonizes demand forecasting with operational planning, ensuring that these insights are translated into actionable strategies.

Sales and Operations Planning (S&OP)

Sales and Operations Planning, commonly referred to as S&OP, is a strategic process where key business functions collaborate to achieve balance between the supply chain's demand and supply side. It is a forward-looking process that aligns an organization's strategic plans with its operational capacity.

At its core, S&OP is about alignment and communication. It serves as a central forum where representatives from sales, marketing, product development, operations, and finance convene to ensure that the organization's operational plans are fully integrated with its commercial objectives.

Typically conducted on a monthly cycle, the S&OP process begins with data gathering and ends with an executive meeting where decisions are ratified and actions are allocated. This cycle involves several steps, including demand review, supply review, pre-S&OP alignment, and the executive S&OP meeting.

During the demand review, sales forecasts are scrutinized, and any discrepancies between the forecasts and actual sales are analyzed. The goal is to create a consensus demand plan that reflects the best estimate of future sales.

Following the demand review, the supply review assesses whether the organization has the resources and capacity to meet the agreed-upon demand plan. It considers production capabilities, inventory levels, supplier performance, and logistics.

Python Code Example: S&OP Inventory Simulation

```python
import numpy as np
import matplotlib.pyplot as plt

# Define initial inventory level and target
initial_inventory = 500
target_inventory = 600

# Simulate demand and production over a 12-month period
np.random.seed(42)
monthly_demand = np.random.normal(loc=50, scale=10, size=12)
monthly_production = np.random.normal(loc=60, scale=5, size=12)
```

```
# Calculate inventory levels
inventory_levels = [initial_inventory]
    inventory_levels.append(max(0, inventory_levels[i] +
monthly_production[i] - monthly_demand[i]))

# Plot the inventory levels
plt.plot(range(13), inventory_levels, marker='o', linestyle='-',
color='b')
plt.axhline(y=target_inventory, color='r', linestyle='--')
plt.title('S&OP Inventory Simulation')
plt.xlabel('Month')
plt.ylabel('Inventory Level')
plt.legend(['Inventory Level', 'Target Inventory'])
plt.show()
` ` `
```

In this simulation, random demand and production figures are generated to visualize how inventory levels fluctuate over time. This kind of modeling can be vital in the S&OP process, helping businesses plan for adequate inventory levels to meet demand.

Pre-S&OP Alignment: Ironing Out Discrepancies

The pre-S&OP step is where the initial reconciliation of supply and demand occurs. This step ensures that any discrepancies are ironed out before the executive S&OP meeting, where strategic decisions are made.

The executive S&OP meeting is the culmination of the process. Here, senior leaders review the proposed plans, make strategic decisions, authorize necessary changes, and allocate resources. The outcome is a balanced and executable plan that aligns with the company's financial goals and market expectations.

A robust S&OP process can lead to a myriad of benefits, including improved customer service levels, optimized inventory management, better new product introductions, and enhanced profitability. It also fosters a culture of collaboration and consensus, which is essential for a responsive and agile supply chain.

The S&OP process complements the demand sensing and shaping strategies discussed earlier. Insights from demand sensing inform the demand review step in S&OP, while demand shaping initiatives can be planned and evaluated within the S&OP framework to ensure they are in line with overall business strategy.

S&OP is not merely a supply chain function; it is a business imperative. It bridges the gap between strategy and execution, ensuring that every part of the organization is synchronized and pulling in the same direction. As businesses navigate the complexities of the modern market, the role of S&OP in driving strategic agility and competitive advantage cannot be overstated.

In the next section, we will explore forecasting accuracy and error analysis, which are critical in assessing the effectiveness of an S&OP process and ensuring continuous improvement.

Forecasting Accuracy and Error Analysis

The pursuit of forecasting accuracy is a relentless endeavor in supply chain management. It's the keystone that supports decision-making processes and, when finely tuned, can significantly reduce operational costs and enhance customer satisfaction. Error analysis, on the other hand, is the diagnostic counterpart that identifies and rectifies the variances between forecasts and actual outcomes.

Forecasting accuracy is a measure of how closely the forecasted values align with the actual data. In the realm of supply chain analytics, the accuracy of demand forecasts is particularly crucial, as it influences inventory levels, production scheduling, and capacity planning.

Quantifying Accuracy: Metrics Matter

```python
return np.mean(np.abs((actual - forecast) / actual)) * 100

# Example usage with actual and forecasted values
actual_sales = np.array([120, 130, 125, 140, 135])
forecasted_sales = np.array([118, 125, 130, 135, 140])

mape = calculate_mape(actual_sales, forecasted_sales)
print(f'MAPE: {mape:.2f}%')
```

This Python function calculates the MAPE, providing a percentage that indicates the average deviation of the forecasted values from the actual data. Lower percentages are indicative of more accurate forecasts.

Error Analysis: The Path to Refinement

Error analysis involves examining the discrepancies between what was predicted and what actually occurred. It requires rigorous investigation and often leads to valuable insights into the dynamics of the supply chain.

Diagnosing Errors through Decomposition

One technique for error analysis is time series decomposition. This method breaks down a time series into its constituent components—trend, seasonality, and residuals—to better understand the underlying patterns and anomalies.

```python
from statsmodels.tsa.seasonal import seasonal_decompose

# Example time series data
data = {'Month': ['Jan', 'Feb', 'Mar', 'Apr', 'May'], 'Sales': [120, 150, 140, 160, 170]}
time_series = pd.Series(data['Sales'], index=pd.to_datetime(data['Month'], format='%b'))

# Decompose the time series
decomposition = seasonal_decompose(time_series, model='additive', period=12)
decomposition.plot()
plt.show()
```

This code snippet demonstrates the decomposition of sales data into trend, seasonal, and residual components. Analyzing these elements separately can help pinpoint specific areas of the forecast that need improvement.

Ongoing monitoring of forecasting accuracy is vital. It allows businesses to respond swiftly to changes in demand patterns and to adjust their models accordingly. Such agility is increasingly necessary in today's volatile market conditions.

Errors in forecasting can have far-reaching consequences, from excess inventory that ties up capital to stockouts that result in lost sales and damaged customer relationships. Accurate forecasts are not just a technical aspiration; they are a commercial necessity.

Advancements in machine learning offer new opportunities to improve forecasting accuracy. Algorithms can process vast amounts of data and identify complex patterns that traditional statistical models may miss. Furthermore, machine learning models can adapt over time, learning from new data to refine their predictions.

Forecasting is inherently an iterative process. With each cycle of S&OP, the forecasts are revised, and the accuracy is evaluated. Error analysis feeds back into the process, informing adjustments to the forecasting models and leading to more accurate predictions.

In the following section, we will delve into real-time data and its implications for demand forecasting, recognizing that the dynamic nature of data can both challenge and enhance the forecasting process.

Real-Time Data and Demand Forecasting

In the echelons of supply chain analytics, real-time data is revolutionizing the way demand forecasting is conducted. It signifies a paradigm shift from traditional batch processing to a dynamic, pulsating flow of information that allows for more nuanced and responsive decision-making.

The incorporation of real-time data into forecasting models enables supply chain professionals to capture the immediacy of market conditions. It's a stark contrast to reliance on historical data alone, which, while valuable, can sometimes lag behind the rapid pace of change in consumer behavior and market trends.

Implementing Real-Time Data Streams

```python
# Python pseudocode for processing real-time data from sensors
import json
import pandas as pd
from kafka import KafkaConsumer

# Set up a Kafka consumer to listen for sensor data
consumer = KafkaConsumer('supply_chain_sensors', bootstrap_servers='sensor_hub:9092')

# Process messages as they arrive
    sensor_data = json.loads(message.value)
    process_sensor_data(sensor_data)

    # Convert sensor data into a pandas DataFrame
    df = pd.DataFrame([data])
    # Implement further processing and integrate into
```

forecasting model

   update_forecast_model(df)

` ` `

This example provides a glimpse into how real-time data might be streamed and processed. It suggests the use of Kafka, a distributed streaming platform, to consume data from supply chain sensors, which is then fed into forecasting models for immediate insight.

The Agility of Adaptive Forecasting

Real-time data empowers organizations to transition to adaptive forecasting models. These models adjust to incoming data streams, allowing for forecasts to be updated continuously. This adaptability is critical in managing unforeseen disruptions or capitalizing on sudden market opportunities.

The impact of real-time data on demand forecasting is profound. It can lead to more accurate replenishment strategies, reduce the risk of stockouts, and optimize inventory turnover. By reacting to real-time signals, companies can align their supply chain operations more closely with current demand.

Despite its benefits, the implementation of real-time data analytics comes with challenges. Data quality and integrity must be maintained to prevent the propagation of errors through the supply chain. Moreover, the sheer volume of data can be overwhelming, necessitating robust data processing and analysis capabilities.

Consider a retailer facing a sudden weather change that triggers an unexpected demand for certain products. With real-time data, they can quickly adjust their inventory levels, reroute logistics, and communicate with suppliers to meet the surge in demand, thus avoiding lost sales and maintaining customer satisfaction.

Real-time data complements the pursuit of forecasting accuracy discussed earlier. By providing immediate feedback, it allows for quicker identification and rectification of forecast errors. It brings a level of precision and responsiveness that static models cannot match.

As we look to the future, the integration of real-time data into Sales and Operations Planning (S&OP) processes will become increasingly standard. It will provide a competitive edge to those who can effectively interpret and act on the wealth of information available.

The utilization of real-time data is a transformative force in demand forecasting. It requires a strategic approach to data management and a willingness to embrace new technologies. As we proceed, we will explore scenario planning and risk assessment, recognizing that the ability to forecast accurately is as much about anticipating change as it is about responding to the present.

Scenario Planning and Risk Assessment in Forecasting

Delving deeper into the realm of demand forecasting, we encounter the strategic tools of scenario planning and risk assessment. These methodologies extend beyond the confines of traditional forecasting, offering a panoramic view that encompasses multiple potential futures and the risks associated with them.

Scenario planning is an exercise in imagination and strategic thinking. It involves constructing a series of plausible future scenarios—narratives based on different combinations of variables and external factors—that could impact the demand for products and services. This approach acknowledges that the future is not a single path but a spectrum of possibilities.

Crafting Scenarios with Data and Insight

```python
import numpy as np
import matplotlib.pyplot as plt

# Define potential market scenarios
scenarios = {
    'expected_case': {'growth_rate': 0.03, 'market_share': 0.25}
}

# Simulate demand for each scenario
    growth_rate = params['growth_rate']
    market_share = params['market_share']
    future_demand = current_demand * (1 + growth_rate) * market_share
    print(f'Scenario: {scenario}, Projected Demand: {future_demand}')

# Plotting the scenarios for visual comparison
demands = [future_demand for future_demand in scenarios.values()]
```

```
plt.bar(scenarios.keys(), demands)
plt.title('Demand Forecasting: Scenario Analysis')
plt.xlabel('Scenarios')
plt.ylabel('Projected Demand')
plt.show()
```
```

This simplified code snippet illustrates how different assumptions about market conditions can be translated into demand projections. Visualizing these projections helps stakeholders understand the possible outcomes and prepare accordingly.

## Risk Assessment: Gauging the Probable and the Impactful

Risk assessment in forecasting seeks to identify and evaluate the risks that could derail expected outcomes. It quantifies not just the likelihood of various events but also their potential impact on the supply chain. This dual focus on probability and impact facilitates more informed decision-making.

## Integrating Risk into Forecasting Models

Modern forecasting models can integrate risk by incorporating probability distributions and stochastic processes, enabling a more nuanced understanding of uncertainty. By factoring in risk, companies can develop contingency plans that mitigate potential adverse effects on the supply chain.

## The Synergy with Real-Time Data

Building on the foundation of real-time data, scenario planning
```

and risk assessment become even more potent. Real-time data allows for the constant recalibration of scenarios and risks, ensuring that plans remain relevant in the face of changing circumstances.

Educating for Risk-Aware Decision Making

A key aspect of employing these techniques is the cultivation of a risk-aware culture within the organization. Stakeholders at all levels must understand the importance of considering various scenarios and the associated risks to make decisions that are both proactive and robust.

Case in Point: Scenario-Driven Strategy Adaptation

Imagine a manufacturer that, through scenario planning, anticipates potential disruptions in the supply of a critical component. By evaluating the risks and developing alternative sourcing strategies in advance, the company can act swiftly when a predicted shortage materializes, thereby maintaining production continuity.

The Future of Forecasting: Dynamic and Informed

As we advance, the integration of scenario planning and risk assessment into forecasting will likely become more sophisticated, driven by advancements in data analytics and computational power. This evolution will enable organizations to not only predict the future but also shape it through strategic actions.

Scenario planning and risk assessment are cornerstones of a forward-looking demand forecasting strategy. They equip supply chain professionals with the foresight and flexibility to navigate an uncertain future, turning unpredictability into a competitive advantage. As we continue to explore the intricacies of supply chain analytics, these tools will remain integral to our understanding of how to build resilient and responsive supply chains.

CHAPTER 4: SUPPLY CHAIN OPTIMIZATION

Linear Programming and Optimization Techniques

In the pursuit of supply chain excellence, linear programming stands out as a mathematical beacon, guiding the way to optimal solutions for complex logistics problems. This technique, a subset of operations research, is pivotal in formulating and solving optimization problems where a linear relationship exists between variables.

Linear programming (LP) is a method used to achieve the best outcome in a mathematical model whose requirements are represented by linear relationships. It's a powerful tool for optimizing resources, reducing costs, and improving efficiency in supply chains.

At its core, LP involves three main components: objective function, constraints, and non-negativity restrictions. The objective function is what needs to be maximized or minimized —such as cost or time. Constraints represent the limitations or requirements of the problem, such as capacity or demand requirements. Non-negativity restrictions ensure that the solution does not contain negative values, which are often nonsensical in the context of a supply chain.

Python and Linear Programming

```python
from scipy.optimize import linprog

# Objective function coefficients (minimize transportation cost)
c = [2, 3, 4] # cost per route

# Inequality constraints matrix (supply and demand constraints)
A = [[1, 1, 0], [0, 1, 1]]
b = [20, 30] # total supply from two warehouses

# Solve the linear programming problem
res = linprog(c, A_ub=A, b_ub=b, method='simplex')

# Output the optimal distribution strategy
print(f'Minimum transportation cost: {res.fun}')
print(f'Optimal route quantities: {res.x}')
```

In this simplified example, the `linprog` function seeks to minimize transportation costs subject to the constraints of supply and demand.

Applications in Supply Chain

- **Determining Optimal Inventory Levels**: By balancing holding costs against stockout risks.

- **Transportation Planning**: Allocating and scheduling shipments to minimize transportation costs while meeting delivery times.

- **Production Scheduling**: Allocating resources to different production tasks to maximize efficiency and throughput.

- **Network Design**: Deciding on the locations and capacities of facilities to balance service levels and logistics costs.

The Role of Sensitivity Analysis

Sensitivity analysis complements LP by assessing how the changes in parameters of the objective function or constraints affect the optimal solution. This analysis is crucial in supply chains where dynamic factors such as fluctuating demand or variable costs can significantly influence the decision-making process.

Consider a company that manufactures a product in multiple factories and must distribute it to various warehouses. LP can be employed to determine the most cost-effective production and distribution plan, taking into account the manufacturing costs, transportation costs, capacities of factories, and demand at warehouses.

Linear programming serves as a fundamental technique in the optimization of supply chain operations. Its capacity to sift through myriad possibilities and pinpoint the most efficient course of action makes it a critical tool in the arsenal of supply chain analytics. Mastery of LP and its applications promises to enhance strategic decision-making and propel supply chains towards greater agility and competitiveness. As we continue to navigate the complexities of supply chain management, the precision and clarity provided by linear programming will undoubtedly remain indispensable.

Network Design and Optimization

Delving deeper into the realm of supply chain optimization, network design emerges as a critical element. It involves configuring the layout of the supply chain network in such a manner that it aligns with the company's strategic objectives. The optimization of this network is a multifaceted challenge, requiring a keen understanding of geography, customer service levels, transportation costs, and the dynamic nature of supply and demand.

Effective network design aims at delivering products and services to customers in the most efficient and timely manner. It involves determining the optimal number and location of production facilities, distribution centers, warehouses, and retail outlets. The design must also consider the capacity of each node and the transportation links between them.

To optimize a supply chain network, one must turn to advanced mathematical models that can evaluate millions of possible configurations. Mixed-integer linear programming (MILP) extends beyond the scope of standard linear programming by allowing for binary variables—useful in decisions that have a yes-or-no outcome, such as whether to open a new facility.

Python's Role in Network Optimization

```python
```

```
from pulp import *

# Define the problem
prob = LpProblem("Supply Chain Network Design", LpMinimize)

# Define binary variables for facility locations
x1 = LpVariable('Facility1', cat='Binary')
x2 = LpVariable('Facility2', cat='Binary')

# Objective function (minimize costs)
prob += 5000 * x1 + 6000 * x2, "Total Facility Costs"

# Constraints (e.g., demand satisfaction)
prob += x1 + x2 >= 1, "Demand Constraint"

# Solve the problem
prob.solve()

# Output the results
    print(v.name, "=", v.varValue)
` ` `
```

This code snippet represents a simplified model where the goal is to minimize the costs of opening facilities while ensuring customer demand is met.

In practice, network design takes into account various trade-offs. For example, a centralized distribution model might reduce inventory holding costs but could increase transportation costs and lead time to customers. Conversely, a decentralized model might bring products closer to the customer but might inflate inventory costs.

Sensitivity Analysis in Network Design

As with linear programming, sensitivity analysis is vital in network design. It assesses the impact of varying input parameters on the network configuration. For instance, a change in fuel prices could shift the balance between different transportation modes, such as trucking versus rail, influencing the overall network design.

Imagine a global enterprise seeking to revamp its distribution network to reduce costs and improve service levels. By applying network optimization models, the company can evaluate different scenarios, such as consolidating warehouses or changing supplier locations, and select the most beneficial strategy.

Network design and optimization are cornerstones of strategic supply chain management. The ability to model and analyze a global network of interconnected activities is not only a competitive advantage but a necessity in today's complex market landscape. Through the power of optimization techniques and tools, businesses can craft a supply chain network that is robust, responsive, and attuned to the ever-evolving demands of the marketplace. The judicious application of these models ensures that the supply chain is not merely a passive conduit for goods but a dynamic engine driving organizational success.

Inventory Optimization Strategies

Inventory optimization is the balancing act of holding just the right amount of inventory to meet demand while minimizing costs associated with excess stock and stockouts. It's a vital component of supply chain management that directly affects the bottom line and customer satisfaction.

Central to inventory optimization is understanding the core principles of inventory management. These include the economic order quantity (EOQ), which determines the optimal order size to minimize total inventory costs, and the reorder point, which signals when it's time to replenish stock based on forecasted demand and lead times.

In today's data-rich environment, sophisticated analytics play an expansive role in inventory management. Predictive analytics can forecast demand more accurately, prescriptive analytics can suggest optimal responses to those forecasts, and descriptive analytics can provide insights into past performance.

Python and Inventory Analysis

```python
import numpy as np

# Define the parameters
annual_demand = 1000
order_cost = 50
holding_cost = 2

# Calculate the Economic Order Quantity (EOQ)
EOQ = np.sqrt((2 * annual_demand * order_cost) / holding_cost)
print(f"The Economic Order Quantity is: {EOQ:.2f}")
```

` ` `

This code computes the EOQ based on the annual demand, the cost of placing an order, and the cost of holding one unit in inventory. It's a fundamental model that informs inventory decision-making.

Leveraging Machine Learning

Machine learning takes inventory optimization further by identifying complex patterns in demand. For example, a random forest algorithm might reveal seasonal trends or the impact of marketing campaigns on inventory levels. Training a model with historical sales data could lead to more nuanced stock policies that anticipate fluctuations in demand.

A practical application of inventory optimization could involve a retailer using machine learning models to predict future sales and adjust inventory levels for each product category. The models could consider factors such as historical sales trends, promotional activities, and external variables like weather patterns.

Advanced inventory strategies such as just-in-time (JIT) and vendor-managed inventory (VMI) rely heavily on the seamless flow of information across the supply chain. JIT minimizes inventory levels by aligning production closely with demand, and VMI shifts the responsibility of managing inventory to suppliers, potentially reducing stockouts and overstock situations.

Sustainability is increasingly important in inventory optimization. By reducing waste and focusing on products' life cycles, companies can not only improve environmental outcomes but also drive efficiency and cost savings. For example, using biodegradable packaging materials can reduce environmental impact, and optimizing inventory levels can minimize waste from unsold products.

Inventory optimization strategies are essential for companies to maintain competitive advantage and customer loyalty. Integrating sophisticated data analysis techniques and Python-based models, businesses can achieve a fine-tuned inventory system that responds adeptly to demand variability, reduces costs, and supports sustainable practices. The continuous improvement of these strategies, powered by technological advancements, will herald a new era of efficiency and responsiveness in supply chain management.

Transportation and Route Optimization

The intricacies of transportation and route optimization represent a cornerstone in the architecture of supply chain efficiency. A meticulously planned route can be the difference between timely delivery and costly delays. At the heart of this optimization lies the quest to deliver goods in the most economically and environmentally sustainable way possible.

Transportation connects the dots in the supply chain, bridging the gap between production and consumption. Optimizing this link involves not only selecting the most direct routes but also considering factors such as fuel costs, driver hours, vehicle maintenance, and changing traffic conditions.

Modern route planning is far from a linear process. It's a multifaceted challenge that requires a blend of historical data analysis, real-time information, and predictive modeling to adapt to ever-shifting variables. The goal is to minimize not just distance and time but also environmental impact and cost.

Python's Contribution to Route Optimization

Python's prowess extends to solving transportation problems through libraries like `networkx`, which can model and analyze complex networks, and `ortools`, a suite of optimization tools developed by Google. These tools can solve the vehicle routing problem (VRP), optimizing the paths taken by a fleet of vehicles to service a set of customers.

```python
from ortools.constraint_solver import routing_enums_pb2
from ortools.constraint_solver import pywrapcp

    data = {}
    data['distance_matrix'] = [
        [0, 2, 9, ...], # distances from point A to others
        [1, 0, 4, ...], # distances from point B to others
        ...
    ]
    data['num_vehicles'] = 3
    data['depot'] = 0
    return data

# Instantiate the data model.
data = create_data_model()

# Create the routing index manager and model.
```

```
manager                                                    =
pywrapcp.RoutingIndexManager(len(data['distance_matrix']),
data['num_vehicles'], data['depot'])
routing = pywrapcp.RoutingModel(manager)

# Solve the VRP.
solution = routing.SolveWithParameters(routing_params)

# A function to print the solution could be added here.
```
` ` `

This snippet initializes a simple route optimization model that minimizes the travel distance for a fleet of vehicles, each starting and ending at a depot.

Incorporating real-time data into route optimization allows for dynamic rerouting in response to traffic conditions, weather events, or last-minute order changes. This agility ensures that the supply chain can react and adapt, minimizing disruptions and maintaining service quality.

Environmental considerations are taking a front seat in route optimization. Fuel-efficient routes, alternative fuel vehicles, and optimization for reduced carbon emissions are becoming common practice. Organizations are using route optimization not only to cut costs but also to achieve sustainability targets.

Beyond the day-to-day routing decisions, strategic transportation management involves long-term analysis of transportation networks. This includes decisions on where to locate new distribution centers, how to allocate resources during peak seasons, and how to structure transportation networks to serve global markets effectively.

Multimodal transportation, which involves using different modes of transport such as shipping, rail, and trucking, offers flexibility and can often lead to significant cost savings and efficiency improvements. Optimization algorithms that can handle the complexities of multimodal logistics are vital for modern supply chains.

As supply chains grow more complex and customer expectations rise, transportation and route optimization is an evolving field that combines data science, logistics expertise, and technology to deliver remarkable efficiencies. Through Python-driven algorithms and a commitment to adaptability and sustainability, businesses can navigate the challenges of the modern transportation landscape, ensuring that deliveries are made on time, costs are managed effectively, and environmental impact is minimized. This ongoing evolution in transportation strategy fortifies the supply chain against disruption and paves the way for a more resilient future.

Cost-to-Serve Optimization

In the intricate web of supply chain operations, the cost-to-serve model stands out as a pivotal concept, one that meticulously dissects the expenses associated with delivering products and services to each customer. It is predicated on the understanding that not all customers are equal in terms of profitability; some may be surprisingly costly to serve, while others contribute significantly to the bottom line.

The journey towards optimizing cost-to-serve begins with the segregation of customers into distinct groups based on various criteria, such as order size, frequency, delivery windows, and service level requirements. This categorization lays the groundwork for understanding the unique cost implications of each segment.

The subsequent step involves a granular analysis of the expense trail left by each customer group. Here, the costs are not merely tallied but scrutinized—from procurement to production, from warehousing to distribution. Every phase of the product's journey is evaluated to identify cost drivers and areas that are ripe for improvement.

For instance, the transportation of goods often reveals considerable opportunities for optimization. By leveraging route planning software, companies can slash fuel costs, reduce delivery times, and improve vehicle utilization rates. Similarly, inventory carrying costs can be mitigated through demand forecasting models that align stock levels with consumption patterns, thereby reducing excess inventory and associated holding costs.

Another facet of cost-to-serve optimization is the strategic application of pricing models. Dynamic pricing strategies, contingent on the cost-to-serve data, allow businesses to adjust the prices based on the service complexity and delivery requirements of different customer groups. This nuanced approach ensures that pricing reflects the true cost of service delivery, safeguarding profit margins.

The implementation of cost-to-serve optimization is not without its challenges. It demands meticulous data collection and robust analytics capabilities. Companies must harness the power of advanced analytics to dissect large volumes of data and extract actionable insights. Python, with its extensive libraries for data analysis, provides an excellent toolkit for this purpose.

Consider a Python script that performs cluster analysis on

customer data, grouping them based on service delivery costs. The script might utilize libraries such as Pandas for data manipulation, Scikit-learn for machine learning algorithms, and Matplotlib for visualizing the results. Through these clusters, a company can discern patterns and outliers, enabling them to formulate tailored strategies for each customer segment.

Through rigorous analysis and strategic implementation, cost-to-serve optimization emerges as a beacon of efficiency, shedding light on the path to enhanced profitability. It is a testament to the transformative power of data analytics in the supply chain, presenting an opportunity for businesses to thrive in a competitive landscape by mastering their cost structures and fortifying their market position.

Multi-Echelon and Global Optimization

Amidst the vast expanse of global commerce, multi-echelon optimization emerges as a critical strategy. This complex and expansive approach to supply chain management acknowledges that a sequence of interrelated decisions must be harmonized across multiple levels, from raw materials to end-consumer delivery. It is the art of synchronizing inventory policies, transportation modalities, and service levels across different echelons in the supply chain to achieve a harmonious balance between cost efficiency and customer service.

In a global context, where supply chains stretch across continents and are subject to diverse market dynamics, the significance of multi-echelon optimization is magnified. It demands an all-encompassing view that considers not only the intricacies of logistics and distribution at each level but also the interdependencies between them. The aim is to create a seamless flow of products, information, and finances across national borders and between multiple facilities such as factories, warehouses, distribution centers, and retail outlets.

Multi-echelon optimization calls for sophisticated mathematical models that can navigate the complexity of global networks. It utilizes algorithms that can simultaneously process a multitude of variables and constraints, such as lead times, variability in demand and supply, transportation costs, and customs regulations. The models are designed to provide decision-makers with insights on how to best position inventory, where to establish hubs, and how to route shipments to minimize costs while ensuring products reach customers swiftly and reliably.

One of the quintessential elements in achieving this optimization is advanced software systems that can process real-time data and provide visibility across all echelons. These systems must be able to analyze vast amounts of data swiftly, drawing from various sources such as ERP systems, transportation management systems, and external market intelligence. The insights gleaned from this data enable businesses to make informed decisions that resonate across the entire supply chain.

Python's role in this endeavor is indispensable, offering a platform for developing custom analytical tools and simulation models. For instance, a Python-based simulation model could be employed to test different network configurations and inventory policies before they're implemented. Libraries like NumPy for numerical computations and SimPy for discrete-event simulation can be used to create these sophisticated models.

Moreover, Python's ability to integrate with other systems and handle large datasets makes it an ideal choice for building the necessary data pipelines for global optimization. It can be used to automate the extraction, transformation, and loading (ETL) processes, ensuring that data from various sources is cleaned, standardized, and ready for analysis. Pandas, for data manipulation, and SQLAlchemy, for database interactions, are examples of the powerful tools available within Python's ecosystem for these tasks.

As companies navigate the ever-evolving landscape of global supply chains, multi-echelon optimization stands as a lighthouse, guiding them through the complexities of modern logistics. By adopting this comprehensive approach, businesses can optimize their operations on a global scale, reducing redundancy, minimizing costs, and enhancing responsiveness. The integration of such optimization techniques into the strategic fabric of supply chain management is not just beneficial but necessary for thriving in today's interconnected world.

Through the lens of multi-echelon and global optimization, we see a world where supply chain efficiency is not just a goal but a dynamic, continuous process. It is an environment where every decision is made with a clear understanding of its ripple effects, ensuring that the global orchestra of supply chain activities plays in perfect harmony.

Sustainability and Green Optimization

As the sun rises on a new era of supply chain management, sustainability and green optimization have become the clarion call for businesses worldwide. The pursuit of efficiency is no longer solely about cost reduction; it has evolved to include the imperative of environmental stewardship. Green optimization in supply chains is an intricate dance of balancing economic goals with ecological responsibility, striving to leave a lighter footprint on the planet while maintaining robust operations.

In the realm of green optimization, the focus is on reducing waste and emissions, conserving energy, and utilizing resources in a manner that promotes longevity and renewability. This approach requires a transformative mindset that considers the entire lifecycle of products and the supply chain's broader impact on ecosystems and communities. By integrating sustainability principles into supply chain operations, companies not only contribute to the health of the planet but also gain a competitive edge through increased efficiency and innovation.

The methodology of green optimization extends to various facets of the supply chain, including product design, material sourcing, manufacturing processes, distribution networks, and end-of-life management. For instance, by designing products with recyclability in mind, companies can ensure that materials are repurposed at the end of their lifecycle, thereby reducing waste. In sourcing, selecting suppliers that adhere to sustainable practices can significantly diminish the environmental impact of raw materials.

Another vital aspect of green optimization is the implementation of energy-efficient technologies and practices within supply chain facilities. From solar panels on warehouse roofs to energy-saving lighting systems, these initiatives not only curtail carbon footprints but also lead to long-term cost savings. Transportation, a major contributor to greenhouse gas emissions, is also a key area for green optimization. Here, route optimization algorithms can minimize fuel consumption, while the transition to electric or hybrid vehicles presents a clear path to reducing emissions.

In the context of analytics, Python serves as a powerful tool for building models that can assess the environmental impact of supply chain decisions. It enables the creation of simulations that take into account various sustainability metrics, such as carbon emissions, water usage, and energy consumption. Python libraries like matplotlib for data visualization and scikit-learn for machine learning can be harnessed to predict outcomes of different green initiatives and optimize supply chain operations accordingly.

The use of Python also facilitates the analysis of big data from supply chain activities to identify inefficiencies and areas where green practices can be implemented. For example, a Python script could analyze logistics data to recommend optimal loading strategies that maximize container space, thereby reducing the number of trips required and cutting down on emissions.

To drive sustainability further, businesses can leverage the Internet of Things (IoT) to monitor and report real-time data on various environmental parameters. Sensors placed throughout the supply chain can collect data on energy usage, resource consumption, and emission levels, which can then be processed using Python to gain insights and facilitate decision-making.

The journey toward sustainable supply chains is not without challenges. It involves navigating complex regulatory environments, aligning diverse stakeholder interests, and investing in new technologies and processes. However, the rewards are substantial, offering a future where supply chains do not just deliver goods but also uphold the principles of environmental sustainability.

As the narrative of supply chains unfolds, green optimization becomes an integral chapter, highlighting that the path to profitability and growth can be aligned with the conservation of our planet's resources. By embedding sustainability into the core strategy of supply chain management, businesses can build resilience, foster innovation, and contribute to a sustainable future for generations to come.

Trade-off Analysis and Decision Making

In the intricate tapestry of supply chain management, trade-off analysis emerges as a pivotal tool, guiding decision-makers through a labyrinth of competing objectives. It is a critical exercise in optimization, where the interplay of cost, quality, speed, and service must be carefully calibrated to achieve the overarching goals of the organization. Trade-off analysis requires a meticulous evaluation of the possible outcomes that each decision might entail, weighing the benefits and drawbacks to arrive at a choice that serves the best interest of both the company and its stakeholders.

As we delve into the nuances of trade-off analysis, we recognize that decisions in the supply chain are seldom straightforward. The allure of lower costs may beckon, but it often comes at the expense of quality or longer lead times. Conversely, prioritizing speed and service can inflate expenses, challenging the financial sustainability of operations. Thus, the art of decision-making in this context is about finding an optimal balance, a harmonious point where the trade-offs are acceptable and the strategic objectives are still met.

The role of analytics in this sphere is to illuminate the path forward with data-driven insights. With the aid of advanced analytical tools, supply chain professionals can model different scenarios, simulate the impact of various decisions, and predict the outcomes with greater accuracy. Python, with its extensive suite of libraries and frameworks, stands as a beacon for those seeking to unravel the complexities of trade-off analysis.

Consider the scenario where a company must decide between multiple suppliers, each offering different terms. A Python-based decision model could be constructed using libraries such as NumPy for numerical computations and pandas for data manipulation. This model could incorporate factors such as cost, delivery times, reliability scores, and capacity constraints, offering a multi-dimensional view of the supplier landscape. By running simulations, decision-makers can visualize the impact of each supplier choice on the supply chain's performance, identifying which trade-offs are most palatable.

Another arena for trade-off analysis is in inventory management, where the conflict between holding costs and service levels frequently arises. Python's optimization libraries, like SciPy, can be employed to determine the ideal inventory levels that balance the risk of stockouts against the cost of excess inventory. These analyses can guide stocking policies and reorder points, ensuring that the supply chain remains responsive without becoming financially burdensome.

Transportation provides yet another domain where trade-off analysis is indispensable. The quest for expedited deliveries must be counterbalanced with the environmental and economic costs of transportation. Python can aid in designing transportation networks that optimize routes and modes of transport, taking into consideration fuel costs, carbon emissions, delivery windows, and vehicle capacities. By employing libraries such as NetworkX for network analysis or OR-Tools for optimization, organizations can envisage the trade-offs inherent in various routing strategies and select the most sustainable and cost-effective options.

Trade-off analysis is not a static process but a dynamic one that adapts to the ever-changing landscape of supply chain dynamics. It demands continuous re-evaluation and adjustment as market conditions fluctuate, new technologies emerge, and customer expectations evolve. The analytical frameworks and models are thus designed not only to solve current dilemmas but also to be scalable and flexible, ready to accommodate the uncertainties of the future.

Ultimately, the decisions made through trade-off analysis define the strategic trajectory of the supply chain. They are the fulcrum upon which the delicate balance of supply chain performance is maintained. By leveraging the power of analytics and the versatility of tools like Python, businesses can navigate these decisions with confidence, knowing that they are equipped to weigh the trade-offs and chart a course that advances their mission while upholding their commitments to customers, shareholders, and the environment.

Continuous Improvement and Kaizen in Supply Chain Optimization

The pursuit of excellence within supply chain operations is a relentless journey, one that is perpetually propelled by the philosophy of continuous improvement, or 'Kaizen.' Originating from the Japanese term for "change for the better," Kaizen is an approach that permeates every facet of an organization, advocating for progressive enhancements over time, no matter how small. In the domain of supply chain optimization, this methodology becomes a catalyst for incremental advances that cumulatively lead to significant enhancements in efficiency, quality, and customer satisfaction.

Kaizen in supply chain optimization is not merely a set of actions but a mindset that encourages employees at all levels to be vigilant for opportunities to refine processes. It is a collaborative effort that thrives on open communication, feedback, and the collective wisdom of the workforce. By fostering an environment where every team member is empowered to suggest improvements, organizations can tap into a wealth of practical insights that might otherwise go unnoticed.

The integration of Kaizen into supply chain practices involves scrutinizing existing operations through a critical lens. Teams are encouraged to identify bottlenecks, eliminate wasteful activities, and streamline workflows. This could involve reconfiguring warehouse layouts for more efficient picking paths, simplifying documentation processes to reduce administrative delays, or implementing cross-training programs to create a more versatile workforce.

Amidst the digital renaissance of supply chains, Kaizen also embraces the application of technology to refine operations. Here, Python emerges as a valuable ally, offering a plethora of libraries and frameworks that can aid in process optimization. For instance, the development of custom algorithms using Python can optimize inventory levels, reducing waste and ensuring that resources are allocated efficiently. Python's data visualization libraries, such as Matplotlib or Seaborn, can be leveraged to create intuitive dashboards that monitor key performance indicators, providing real-time feedback and highlighting areas ripe for improvement.

Continuous improvement is inherently data-driven, relying on a constant influx of information to guide decision-making. Within a Kaizen-centric supply chain, data analytics becomes the compass that directs efforts towards the most impactful interventions. By analyzing historical performance data, supply chain managers can identify patterns and trends that pinpoint inefficiencies. Python's machine learning capabilities, facilitated by libraries like scikit-learn, can be harnessed to predict future bottlenecks and preemptively address them, maintaining the momentum of improvement.

A quintessential element of Kaizen in supply chain optimization is the concept of 'Gemba,' the Japanese term for "the real place." In practice, this means going to the heart of where work happens – the warehouse floor, the loading dock, the manufacturing line – to observe processes firsthand and gain a deeper understanding of the operational realities. These Gemba walks are instrumental in identifying areas that may benefit from technological upgrades or process re-engineering, ensuring that improvements are grounded in actual operational contexts.

Moreover, Kaizen emphasizes the principle that no process is ever perfect, and there is always room for enhancement. It instills a culture of agility, where supply chain operations are continuously reviewed and adapted to meet the shifting demands of the market and to capitalize on emerging opportunities. Whether it's refining supplier selection criteria, adopting greener packaging materials, or improving delivery schedules, the spirit of Kaizen keeps the supply chain in a state of perpetual evolution, always striving for better.

The integration of continuous improvement and Kaizen into supply chain optimization is a strategic choice that yields dividends in operational excellence. It is a journey that requires patience, persistence, and a proactive stance towards change. By embracing Kaizen, supply chains can not only optimize their current operations but also build a resilient foundation that supports long-term growth and innovation. Through the thoughtful application of analytics and the harnessing of technologies like Python, the continuous improvement process becomes an ingrained feature of the supply chain, driving it towards new horizons of efficiency and effectiveness.

Simulation and Digital Twins in Supply Chain Optimization

In the contemporary theatre of supply chain management, simulation and digital twins stand out as revolutionary tools, redefining the boundaries of what can be achieved in optimization. Simulation is the art of mirroring real-world processes in a virtual environment to test and analyze the outcomes of various scenarios without the risk of disrupting actual operations. A digital twin, on the other hand, is a dynamic, digital replica of a physical system that updates and changes alongside its real-world counterpart, offering unparalleled insight into the system's performance and potential points of improvement.

Simulation in supply chain optimization provides a sandbox for managers to play out 'what-if' scenarios. By creating a model of the supply chain within a computer program, one can explore the consequences of changes ranging from minor adjustments to monumental shifts in strategy. For instance, how would a change in supplier impact delivery times and costs? What would be the effect of a sudden spike in demand on inventory levels? Simulation software allows for these questions and more to be explored in depth, without the cost or risk of real-world experimentation.

Digital twins take this concept a step further by not only enabling simulation of scenarios but also providing an ongoing, real-time reflection of the supply chain. By integrating data from various sources, including IoT devices, enterprise resource planning (ERP) systems, and customer feedback, digital twins offer a living model that can be used for continuous optimization. They allow companies to monitor their supply chain in real-time and simulate adjustments in a virtual environment to predict and prevent potential issues before they manifest in reality.

One can imagine the digital twin of a warehouse that tracks inventory levels, shipment arrivals and departures, and employee movements. By applying analytics to this data, the system can identify inefficiencies such as frequently travelled routes that could be shortened or times when the warehouse is underutilized. Python's role in this scenario is pivotal. Its powerful data processing libraries, such as Pandas and NumPy, can handle the massive streams of data generated by digital twins, while simulation frameworks like SimPy can model complex supply chain networks.

Moreover, digital twins can be equipped with machine learning algorithms to forecast future states of the supply chain based on historical data, allowing companies to proactively manage risks and capitalize on upcoming opportunities. Python's vast ecosystem, with libraries like TensorFlow and PyTorch, provides the necessary tools for building predictive models that can turn the digital twin into a prescient oracle of supply chain operations.

The implementation of simulation and digital twins does not solely reside in the realm of large corporations. Small and medium-sized enterprises can also benefit from these technologies. Cloud-based simulation and digital twin services offer affordable and scalable solutions that fit the needs and budgets of smaller businesses, democratizing access to these advanced optimization tools.

As we cast our gaze towards the future, the convergence of simulation and digital twins with other technologies such as blockchain for secure data sharing, and augmented reality for immersive interaction, suggests a horizon brimming with possibilities for supply chain optimization. These technologies are not mere tools but partners that collaborate with supply chain managers to unveil novel solutions and strategies that can lead to breakthroughs in efficiency, cost reduction, and customer satisfaction.

In embracing the synergy of simulation and digital twins, businesses can construct a resilient, responsive, and intelligent supply chain. This digital convergence acts as a linchpin for strategic decision-making, offering a depth of insight that was once the stuff of dreams. It is through these lenses that the supply chain can be viewed not just as a sequence of activities, but as a dynamic ecosystem ripe for innovation and ripe for optimization, shaped by the meticulous application of technology and analytical foresight.

CHAPTER 5: SUPPLY CHAIN VISIBILITY AND MONITORING

Defining Supply Chain Visibility

E mbarking upon the quest to define supply chain visibility, one must consider it as the cornerstone of modern supply chain management. It is the ability to track products and components from the manufacturer to the final destination in near-real-time. Visibility is not merely about observing the flow of goods; it is about understanding and managing the intricate web of supply chain activities to ensure efficiency, responsiveness, and customer satisfaction.

At its core, supply chain visibility provides a transparent view of the inventory levels, production schedules, shipment information, and all other processes involved in the supply chain. It allows stakeholders to pinpoint exactly where goods are at any given moment, predict when they will arrive at their next destination, and prepare for their arrival. This level of insight is critical in an era where consumers demand faster delivery times and more information about the products they purchase.

Python plays a significant role in achieving such visibility. For instance, Python's ability to interact with APIs allows for the seamless aggregation of tracking data from different carriers into a centralized system. Libraries like Requests can automate the retrieval of shipment status from logistics providers, while JSON or XML libraries parse this data into a structured format that's ready for analysis.

Furthermore, supply chain visibility is not just about tracking physical goods; it's equally about the flow of information. The ability to access and analyze data from across the supply chain enables better decision-making. Python's data analysis libraries, such as Pandas, allow for the manipulation and analysis of large datasets, which can be used to generate insights into lead times, bottleneck identification, and supplier performance.

The true power of visibility lies in its proactive nature. When a company has a clear line of sight across its supply chain, it can anticipate problems before they occur. For example, if a shipment is delayed, the system can alert relevant parties to take corrective action, such as rerouting shipments or adjusting production schedules. This proactive stance is bolstered by Python's forecasting libraries, like Statsmodels or Facebook's Prophet, which can model future supply chain scenarios based on current data.

Implementing a robust supply chain visibility platform can also have far-reaching implications for risk management. By having detailed insights into each link of the supply chain, companies can identify potential risks and vulnerabilities and develop strategies to mitigate them. Python's versatility in data modelling and risk assessment can facilitate the creation of risk management dashboards that provide an overview of risk factors and their potential impact on the supply chain.

Moreover, visibility is not confined to the internal workings of a company. It extends to external partners, suppliers, and customers, creating a collaborative environment where information is shared freely and securely. This level of collaboration can lead to more synchronized and efficient supply chains that benefit all parties involved.

The future advancements in supply chain visibility are poised to integrate even more sophisticated technologies. Machine learning algorithms can predict and adapt to changing conditions, while IoT devices provide granular detail on the status and condition of goods in transit. These developments are set to redefine what is possible in supply chain management, with visibility being the lynchpin that connects the physical flow of goods with the digital flow of information.

Supply chain visibility is the panoramic view that companies need in today's complex and fast-paced global economy. It is the foundation upon which resilient and agile supply chains are built, empowering businesses with the clarity and confidence to navigate the most challenging of market conditions. Through the strategic implementation of technology, including the adept use of Python for data analysis and integration, organizations can transform their supply chains into transparent, efficient, and customer-centric operations.

Real-Time Tracking and Monitoring Systems

Real-time tracking and monitoring systems are the sinews that give supply chain visibility its strength and agility. These systems are the technological marvels that allow businesses to gather, analyze, and act upon data as events unfold throughout the supply chain. They are the eyes and ears of the operation, providing a continuous stream of information that keeps all stakeholders informed and ready to respond to any situation.

The essence of real-time tracking lies in the constellation of technologies that make dynamic monitoring possible. GPS, for instance, has become a standard for geolocation tracking of vehicles. This information, when integrated with a Python-based system using libraries like Folium for mapping, can provide an interactive, real-time visual representation of a product's journey across the globe.

Another crucial aspect of these systems is the Internet of Things (IoT), which allows for the interconnection of physical devices within the supply chain. Sensors placed on containers, pallets, or individual products can transmit data about location, temperature, humidity, and other environmental conditions. This data becomes invaluable when ensuring the integrity of perishable goods or sensitive equipment. Python's role in IoT is often in the backend, where frameworks like Flask or Django can process the data received from devices and display it on a user interface.

Radio-frequency identification (RFID) technology also plays a pivotal role in real-time tracking. Unlike traditional barcodes, RFID tags can be scanned without line-of-sight and can store more data. By leveraging Python's libraries to work with RFID data, supply chain managers can gain insights into inventory levels and product movement within warehouses and retail environments, all in real-time.

Cloud-based platforms are central to the effectiveness of these systems. They allow for the storage and processing of vast amounts of data while providing access to this information from any location with an internet connection. Python's compatibility with cloud services like AWS, Azure, and Google

Cloud makes it an excellent tool for developing scalable real-time tracking solutions.

Moreover, real-time tracking and monitoring systems are not solely about observing; they are about responding. Advanced systems incorporate features such as automated alerts and notifications. For example, a Python script can be programmed to send an email or SMS alert when a shipment deviates from its planned route or when a storage condition falls outside of set parameters. This allows for immediate actions to be taken, minimizing the impact of disruptions.

Let's consider a practical example where Python's capabilities shine. A supply chain manager wants to implement a system that not only tracks shipments but also predicts estimated time of arrival (ETA) more accurately. By using machine learning libraries like scikit-learn or TensorFlow, a Python-based application could analyze historical data on traffic patterns, weather conditions, and driver performance to provide a more precise ETA for shipments.

As the supply chain's environment becomes more volatile and customer expectations rise, the importance of real-time tracking and monitoring systems becomes even more pronounced. They are not just tools for overseeing operations; they are integral to a proactive approach to supply chain management. In an age where delays and disruptions can significantly impact customer satisfaction and the bottom line, these systems offer a way to maintain control and ensure a smooth, uninterrupted flow of goods and information.

In this realm of constant motion and flux, the implementation of real-time tracking and monitoring systems is not just a luxury—it is a necessity. It enables businesses to maintain a competitive edge by offering high levels of service and responsiveness. By harnessing the power of Python and the latest in tracking technologies, companies can build robust, responsive, and resilient supply chains capable of meeting the demands of the modern economy.

Dashboards and Control Towers

To navigate the complexities of contemporary supply chains, managers need command centers that offer both a panoramic view and the ability to zero in on specific details—the role served by dashboards and control towers. These sophisticated hubs of information transform raw data into actionable insights, which are essential for making informed decisions rapidly.

Dashboards are visual interfaces that present the most critical metrics in an easily digestible format. They are the bridge between the vast data oceans and the strategic decisions that steer the supply chain. By utilizing Python's powerful data visualization libraries such as Matplotlib, Seaborn, or Plotly, analysts can construct interactive and real-time dashboards that highlight key performance indicators (KPIs). This can include data on inventory levels, shipping statuses, and supplier performance, among others.

Control towers take the concept of dashboards further by integrating diverse data streams to provide comprehensive visibility and facilitate cross-functional decision-making. They are akin to an air traffic control tower, where a multitude of data points converge to give a single, unified view of all supply chain activities. These towers enable managers to anticipate problems, identify bottlenecks, and respond proactively to any issues that arise. Python's ability to handle large datasets with tools like pandas and its compatibility with real-time data processing makes it an ideal language for building the backbone of control towers.

Within these systems, exception management is a crucial component. By setting thresholds for performance metrics, a control tower can flag any anomalies that deviate from the norm. A Python-based system can automate this process, generating alerts when, for example, a shipment's delivery status falls into jeopardy. These alerts prompt supply chain managers to take swift corrective action, thus reducing potential delays and enhancing overall efficiency.

Scenario analysis is another feature that control towers often employ. By integrating predictive analytics, they can simulate various supply chain scenarios, such as the impact of a new supplier or a change in shipping routes. Python's libraries for machine learning and statistical analysis, like NumPy and SciPy, enable the creation of these predictive models, helping managers to evaluate the potential outcomes of different decisions before committing to a course of action.

Dashboards and control towers also serve as collaborative platforms. They facilitate communication between different departments and partners by providing a shared view of the supply chain. This shared view ensures that everyone is on the same page, working with the same information, and moving towards the same objectives. In this collaborative space, Python's support for web development, through frameworks like Django, can be utilized to create secure, multi-user environments where stakeholders can interact with the data and with each other.

For example, let's imagine a scenario where a sudden spike in demand for a product is detected. A control tower, equipped with a Python-powered dashboard, can instantly display this trend, allowing supply chain partners to see the surge in real-time. The demand spike triggers an automated workflow, also designed in Python, which assesses inventory levels, predicts the required production increase, and communicates with suppliers to ensure that the additional materials are procured swiftly.

Additionally, these systems can integrate with customer relationship management (CRM) platforms to provide a view of the customer's experience. From order placement to delivery, dashboards can track the customer's journey, offering insights into service levels and identifying opportunities to enhance the customer experience.

Dashboards and control towers are indispensable in the digital arsenal of supply chain analytics. They provide the strategic vantage point from which supply chain managers can oversee their domain with clarity and precision. By leveraging the versatility of Python to process, analyze, and visualize data, these tools empower businesses to manage their operations proactively, adapt to changing conditions, and uphold the promise of delivering the right product, to the right place, at the right time.

Internet of Things (IoT) in Supply Chain Visibility

The Internet of Things (IoT) has revolutionized the landscape of supply chain management by embedding intelligence into physical objects. This seamless blend of the digital and physical worlds offers unprecedented levels of visibility throughout the supply chain. IoT devices, ranging from sensors to RFID tags, collect and transmit real-time data, painting a dynamic and granular picture of every asset's status and location.

Consider the transformative impact of IoT on inventory management. Traditional methods rely heavily on manual counts and are prone to error. In contrast, IoT-enabled systems provide continuous, automated updates on stock levels. Smart shelves equipped with weight sensors can detect inventory changes in real-time, triggering automatic replenishments through Python-scripted inventory management applications. This not only ensures optimal stock levels but also reduces the risk of overstocking or stockouts.

Transportation and logistics also benefit from IoT's capabilities. Goods fitted with GPS trackers transmit their location, allowing for real-time tracking of shipments. Temperature sensors can monitor the conditions of sensitive cargo, such as pharmaceuticals or perishable goods, ensuring they are transported within safe parameters. Python's ability to integrate with IoT platforms means that the data collected by these sensors can be processed and analyzed to provide actionable insights. For instance, a Python-based analysis could predict potential delays due to weather conditions and suggest alternative routes, thereby improving on-time delivery rates.

Moreover, IoT facilitates predictive maintenance of supply chain equipment. Sensors on machines can report performance data, which, when fed into Python-powered predictive models, can forecast potential equipment failures. This allows maintenance to be performed just in time, reducing downtime and extending the life of the equipment.

A practical example of IoT in action can be seen in warehouse management. IoT sensors track the movement of goods within the facility, while automated guided vehicles (AGVs) transport products efficiently. Python algorithms can be used to analyze traffic patterns within the warehouse and optimize the routes taken by AGVs, minimizing congestion and improving throughput.

On the sustainability front, IoT devices help monitor the environmental impact of supply chain activities. Sensors can track energy consumption, waste production, and emissions across the supply chain, feeding data into Python-based sustainability dashboards. These dashboards can help companies identify areas where they can reduce their environmental footprint and meet their sustainability goals.

IoT also enhances collaboration across the supply chain network. By sharing IoT-generated data with partners, companies can improve coordination and responsiveness. For example, a supplier might access IoT data to understand a manufacturer's inventory levels better, thereby adjusting production schedules to align with demand.

In essence, the Internet of Things empowers supply chain professionals with a level of visibility that was previously unattainable. It unlocks a world where every element of the supply chain is interconnected and communicative, providing a rich tapestry of data that, when harnessed through the analytical power of Python, can optimize operations, reduce costs, and deliver a superior customer experience.

As we advance into the future, the synergy between IoT and supply chain analytics will continue to deepen, paving the way for even more sophisticated, responsive, and intelligent supply chain management practices.

RFID, Barcodes, and Other Tracking Technologies

The digitization of the supply chain is incomplete without

discussing the pivotal role played by RFID, barcodes, and a myriad of tracking technologies. These tools are the foundational elements that enable the granular tracking and identification of items as they journey through various stages of the supply chain.

RFID, or Radio-Frequency Identification, uses electromagnetic fields to automatically identify and track tags attached to objects. The tags contain electronically stored information which can be read from a distance, eliminating the need for direct line-of-sight scanning that barcodes require. This technology has been a game-changer in asset tracking and inventory management. For instance, in a retail environment, RFID tags attached to garments enable real-time inventory visibility, drastically reducing the time taken for stock-taking and enhancing the accuracy of inventory records.

Barcodes, despite being an older technology, remain ubiquitous in the supply chain due to their simplicity and cost-effectiveness. Every barcode is unique and encodes information that can be quickly scanned and interpreted by a computer system. The integration of barcode scanning with Python-based inventory management systems allows for efficient data capture and management. An illustrative example is the point-of-sale systems in retail stores, where scanning a product's barcode can instantly retrieve price information and update inventory levels.

Beyond RFID and barcodes, other tracking technologies are increasingly being used. GPS, for instance, offers wide-area tracking capabilities essential for monitoring vehicles and shipments across long distances. Combined with Python's data visualization libraries, such as Matplotlib or Seaborn, GPS data can be transformed into interactive maps and dashboards, providing a clear view of logistical networks and shipment statuses.

NFC, or Near Field Communication, is another technology that offers contactless identification and has found its niche in secure transactions and consumer engagement. In supply chains, NFC can be used in tandem with mobile technologies to enhance the ease of operations, particularly in confirming the authenticity of products and facilitating secure access to warehouses and restricted areas.

Emerging technologies like BLE (Bluetooth Low Energy) beacons are also finding their place in the supply chain. These small devices transmit signals that can be picked up by smartphones or other BLE-enabled devices, enabling indoor location tracking and navigation. In a large distribution center, BLE beacons can help workers quickly locate items, thereby reducing the time spent on picking and packing processes.

The convergence of these tracking technologies with analytics platforms has led to the development of complex event processing systems. These systems, often powered by Python's advanced computational capabilities, can interpret the data from multiple tracking sources, identify patterns, and trigger appropriate responses. For example, if an RFID system flags an inventory discrepancy, a Python script can automatically adjust reorder levels or initiate an audit process.

In terms of enhancing visibility, these tracking technologies are not just about knowing where an item is. They are about understanding the journey of the product, the conditions it has been exposed to, and the efficiency of the processes it has undergone. With the analysis of tracking data, organizations can optimize their supply chain operations, reduce errors, and improve service levels.

To illustrate, consider a pharmaceutical company that needs to ensure its products are stored within specific temperature ranges. RFID tags with temperature sensors can continuously monitor and record temperature data. If the temperature deviates from the acceptable range, a Python-based monitoring system can instantly alert the quality control team to take corrective action, thereby safeguarding the integrity of the pharmaceutical products.

RFID, barcodes, and other tracking technologies form the nervous system of the supply chain, transmitting vital information that keeps the operations running smoothly. When integrated with robust analytics, they not only provide visibility but also empower businesses to be proactive in their decision-making. As the demand for transparency and speed in the supply chain escalates, these technologies will undoubtedly evolve, offering even richer data and insights that drive efficiency and innovation.

Exception Management and Alert Systems

In the seamless flow of supply chain operations, exceptions are the rule. As such, robust exception management and alert systems are vital to ensure that these disruptions are addressed swiftly and efficiently, minimizing their impact on the overall supply chain performance.

An exception in supply chain context refers to any event that deviates from the planned process or expected outcome. These can range from delayed shipments, inventory shortages, to quality issues. The key to managing these exceptions is not just to react to them, but to anticipate and plan for them.

Exception management systems are designed to detect, analyze, and respond to these unplanned events. They function by setting predefined rules and parameters that, when breached, trigger alerts. These alerts notify the relevant personnel so that immediate action can be taken. For example, if a shipment is expected to arrive at a distribution center by a certain time and it doesn't, the system would flag this as an exception and send an alert to the logistics manager.

At the heart of these systems is often a powerful analytics engine, frequently developed with Python, which can process large volumes of data in real-time, identify patterns of exceptions, and predict potential issues before they occur. Python's extensive libraries such as Pandas for data analysis and SciPy for scientific and technical computing enable complex computations that can sift through noise and highlight significant anomalies.

Alert systems must be carefully calibrated to balance sensitivity and specificity. If the thresholds for alerts are set too low, the system may generate an excessive number of false alarms, leading to 'alert fatigue' where users begin to ignore notifications. Conversely, if thresholds are too high, critical exceptions may go unnoticed. Therefore, fine-tuning these systems is a continuous process that benefits greatly from machine learning algorithms. Python's machine learning libraries, like Scikit-learn, allow the development of models that can learn from historical data and improve the accuracy of exception detection over time.

Moreover, the integration of these systems with mobile technology ensures that alerts can be received and acted upon no matter where the stakeholders are. This mobility is crucial in modern supply chains, which are characterized by their fast pace and global reach. With Python's cross-platform capabilities and frameworks such as Kivy, developers can create applications that send real-time notifications to users' smartphones or tablets, ensuring prompt response to any issue.

The advantages of an efficient exception management and alert system are manifold. They help in maintaining service levels by reducing the downtime caused by exceptions. They also contribute to better customer satisfaction as issues can be resolved before they affect the end user. Internally, they promote a proactive culture where teams are encouraged to address the root causes of exceptions rather than merely dealing with their consequences.

A practical application of such a system could be seen in a manufacturing context, where a sudden machine breakdown on the assembly line can cause significant delays. An alert system with integrated predictive maintenance capabilities, powered by Python's statistical modeling, could preemptively warn the maintenance team about the likelihood of a machine failure, based on data such as vibration analysis or temperature readings. This can lead to timely maintenance work before the breakdown occurs, ensuring that production runs smoothly with minimal interruptions.

In essence, exception management and alert systems are an indispensable part of modern supply chain operations, acting as sentinels that guard against the unforeseen. By leveraging the power of Python and its analytics prowess, these systems not only mitigate risks but also transform the way organizations respond to the inevitable variances that occur within the supply chain. They enable a shift from reactive to predictive management, where businesses are not caught off guard by exceptions but are prepared and equipped to handle them with agility and insight.

End-to-End Visibility and Transparency

In a world where supply chains stretch across continents and markets demand ever-faster delivery times, the imperative for end-to-end visibility and transparency in supply chain operations has never been greater. Achieving this level of clarity is not merely about keeping tabs on products and components as they move from supplier to customer; it's about constructing a supply chain that is as transparent as crystal, capable of reflecting real-time data at every twist and turn.

End-to-end visibility refers to the ability to track every element of the supply chain journey, from raw materials to finished products, as they progress through various stages: procurement, manufacturing, distribution, and delivery. Transparency complements this by providing all stakeholders with access to this information, ensuring that no data is obscured or withheld.

The benefits of such a system are profound. For one, it allows companies to respond with alacrity to changes in demand or supply, as they possess the information needed to make swift, informed decisions. Moreover, this transparency fosters trust among all parties involved—suppliers, manufacturers, distributors, and customers—establishing a foundation for stronger, more resilient business relationships.

Python plays a crucial role in creating these visibility systems. Its versatility in handling APIs allows it to connect disparate systems across the supply chain, aggregating data into a centralized platform. For instance, Python's Requests library can facilitate the retrieval of tracking information from third-party logistics providers, while its JSON library can parse this data into a human-readable format.

The cornerstone of end-to-end visibility lies in the judicious application of technology. Radio-frequency identification (RFID) and global positioning systems (GPS) are just two of the tools that feed data into supply chain systems, offering a granular level of detail about the location and status of items. Python's role here extends to analyzing this data, utilizing libraries like Matplotlib for visualizing complex datasets, making it easier for decision-makers to digest and act upon.

The concept of a 'digital twin'—a virtual model of the physical supply chain—is becoming an increasingly popular tool for achieving transparency. By simulating the real-world supply chain in a digital space, companies can test and predict outcomes, plan for contingencies, and optimize operations without risking real-world assets. Python's computational capabilities are ideal for creating these sophisticated models, with libraries such as NumPy and SimPy enabling detailed simulations of supply chain dynamics.

However, implementing this level of visibility and transparency is not without its challenges. It requires a robust IT infrastructure, capable of capturing and communicating vast amounts of data quickly and securely. It also necessitates a cultural shift within organizations, where data sharing is encouraged, and silos are broken down. The integration of supply chain partners into this transparent ecosystem is equally critical, as the chain is only as strong as its weakest link.

A case in point is the food industry, where consumers increasingly demand to know the provenance of the items they purchase. A transparent supply chain can provide this information, tracking produce from farm to fork. Python can assist by analyzing data from various sources—farmers, transporters, retailers—and presenting it in a consumer-friendly format, perhaps through a mobile app or website, thereby enhancing the customer experience and reinforcing the brand's commitment to transparency.

End-to-end visibility and transparency are not just beneficial; they are essential for a modern, responsive supply chain. By harnessing the power of Python and other technologies, companies can illuminate every corner of their supply chain, ensuring that they are not just participants in the market, but leaders setting the standard for operational excellence.

Supplier Performance and Compliance Monitoring

To navigate the complexities of modern supply chains, businesses must ensure that their suppliers adhere to agreed-upon standards of performance and compliance. Monitoring these aspects is pivotal, as it directly influences the quality, efficiency, and ethical standards of the end-to-end supply chain.

Supplier performance monitoring is an expansive term encompassing the assessment of a supplier's ability to meet delivery deadlines, maintain product quality, and uphold service level agreements. Compliance monitoring extends this scope to include adherence to legal regulations, environmental guidelines, and labor laws. Together, these mechanisms form a bulwark that safeguards the integrity of the supply chain.

Python's analytical prowess is indispensable in supplier performance and compliance monitoring. With the aid of its extensive libraries, like pandas for data manipulation and SciPy for advanced computations, analysts can process and interpret supplier data efficiently. This could involve creating scorecards that evaluate suppliers based on various key performance indicators (KPIs) such as on-time delivery rate, defect rate, and response time to issues.

One of the most salient features of a robust monitoring system is the ability to predict potential disruptions or non-compliance before they escalate into larger issues. Here, Python's machine learning capabilities come to the forefront. Utilizing libraries such as scikit-learn, businesses can build predictive models that forecast supplier performance based on historical data, allowing for proactive measures rather than reactive ones.

At the heart of monitoring lies the collection and analysis of data from various touchpoints with suppliers. For instance, Python scripts can be written to automatically pull data from enterprise resource planning (ERP) systems, supplier portals, and even social media to gauge supplier reliability and public perception. This data amalgamation provides a comprehensive picture that informs the monitoring process.

Illustrating the practical application of these concepts, consider a manufacturer that sources components from multiple global suppliers. By implementing a Python-driven dashboard that consolidates real-time data on supplier performance and compliance, the manufacturer can swiftly identify anomalies. Should a supplier begin to consistently miss deadlines or receive reports of regulatory breaches, the dashboard can trigger alerts, prompting immediate action. Moreover, the dashboard could incorporate geospatial analysis using libraries like Geopandas to visualize the global spread of suppliers and potential risks associated with geopolitical events.

Compliance monitoring can be particularly nuanced, as regulations often vary by region and industry. Python can help navigate this complexity by parsing through legislative documents and regulatory updates, using natural language processing (NLP) techniques from libraries like NLTK or spaCy, to extract relevant information and compare it against supplier practices.

Furthermore, the integration of blockchain technology into the supply chain offers an immutable record of transactions and interactions with suppliers, enhancing traceability and accountability. Python's blockchain libraries, such as PyChain, could be leveraged to develop systems that ensure and verify compliance across the entire network of suppliers.

Implementing these systems requires not just technological prowess but also cross-functional collaboration within the organization. Stakeholders from procurement, quality assurance, and compliance departments need to align on the metrics and thresholds that define acceptable performance and compliance levels. It is a concerted effort that, when executed well, can significantly mitigate risk and enhance the overall value delivered by the supply chain.

In essence, supplier performance and compliance monitoring is an ongoing process, vital to maintaining a supply chain that is both resilient and in good standing. Through the strategic use of Python and its libraries, companies can establish a dynamic, responsive system that not only tracks the current state of supplier affairs but also anticipates future trends and prepares for them with foresight and agility.

Customer-Centric Visibility Strategies

In a marketplace where customer satisfaction is paramount, visibility strategies must evolve to center around the end consumer's experience. Customer-centric visibility is about ensuring that clients have clear insights into the status of their orders, inventory levels, and delivery timelines. It's a strategic approach that not only enhances transparency but also builds trust and loyalty by placing the customer's needs at the forefront of supply chain operations.

A customer-centric visibility strategy leverages technology to provide real-time updates and proactive communication throughout the customer journey. This includes the integration of systems that allow customers to track their orders from placement to delivery. Such integrations can be facilitated by Python, through its robust web development frameworks like Django or Flask, which enable the creation of customer portals with live tracking functionalities.

Python's role extends to the backend, where it processes vast streams of data from various points in the supply chain. Using data analytics libraries like NumPy and pandas, businesses can extract meaningful insights from this data and present it to customers in an understandable format. For example, a Python script might analyze shipping data to predict delivery windows with greater accuracy, which can then be communicated to the customer, setting realistic expectations and reducing uncertainty.

A pivotal component of customer-centric visibility is the ability to promptly address and resolve issues as they arise. This demands a system that not only monitors the supply chain but also facilitates rapid response and resolution workflows. Python can aid in this by automating the detection of potential delays or inventory shortages and triggering the necessary alerts to service teams. This proactive stance ensures that customers are informed of potential issues before they become significant problems, reinforcing the company's commitment to customer service.

Moreover, Python's machine learning capabilities can be utilized to personalize the customer experience. Algorithms can analyze past purchasing behaviors and preferences to tailor the visibility offered to individual customers. For instance, customers who frequently order time-sensitive products may receive more frequent updates about their shipments, or be given priority in the event of limited stock availability.

In the digital age, social media platforms have become a critical touchpoint for customer engagement. Python's ability to interface with social media APIs allows companies to monitor customer sentiment and feedback in real time. Sentiment analysis, performed using NLP libraries like TextBlob or Gensim, can interpret customer posts and messages to gauge satisfaction levels and identify areas for improvement in the supply chain visibility strategy.

Another innovative application of Python in enhancing customer-centric visibility is the creation of interactive dashboards using libraries such as Plotly or Dash. These dashboards can be customer-facing, offering a visual representation of the supply chain's performance in relation to their orders. They can show inventory levels, estimated delivery times, and even the environmental impact of their purchases, catering to the growing consumer demand for sustainable practices.

To effectively implement a customer-centric visibility strategy, supply chain managers must ensure that internal and external systems are seamlessly integrated. This can involve the synchronization of warehouse management systems (WMS), transportation management systems (TMS), and customer relationship management (CRM) platforms. Through the use of Python's versatile scripting, these integrations become smoother, allowing for a unified view that benefits both the supply chain operators and the customers they serve.

Embracing a customer-centric visibility strategy is not merely about adopting new technologies; it's about cultivating a culture that values transparency and responsiveness. It requires a shift in perspective wherein every member of the supply chain, from suppliers to logistics providers, is aligned with the end goal of delivering exceptional customer service. With Python as a technological ally, businesses can develop visibility solutions that not only meet but exceed customer expectations, fostering a competitive edge in an increasingly demanding marketplace.

Analytics for Predictive Visibility

The advent of analytics in supply chain management has ushered in an era where foresight is as critical as insight. Predictive visibility stands at the forefront of this paradigm shift, empowering businesses to anticipate and respond to potential supply chain disruptions before they escalate into customer-facing issues. It's an analytical approach that uses historical data, statistical algorithms, and machine learning techniques to forecast future events, ensuring that companies can stay one step ahead of demand and supply fluctuations.

Predictive visibility goes beyond traditional tracking; it's about harnessing the power of predictive analytics to enhance decision-making and operational efficiency. Python, with its extensive ecosystem of data science libraries, is an instrumental tool in developing predictive models that can analyze patterns and trends within supply chain data. Libraries such as scikit-learn and TensorFlow provide the necessary infrastructure to build robust predictive models capable of forecasting demand, identifying potential delays, and optimizing inventory levels.

One practical application of predictive visibility is in demand forecasting. By analyzing historical sales data, promotional schedules, and external factors such as market trends and seasonal variations, Python's predictive models can generate accurate demand projections. These forecasts allow supply chains to adjust their production schedules, manage inventory more efficiently, and minimize the risk of stockouts or excess inventory.

Another area where predictive visibility is transformative is in risk management. Using Python to perform risk analysis, supply chain managers can identify and evaluate the probability of various risks, such as supplier failures, transport delays, or natural disasters. By integrating these risk assessments into their planning, companies can develop contingency strategies to mitigate the impact of such events. Python's simulation capabilities, enabled by libraries like SimPy, can model different scenarios to help managers understand the potential outcomes and prepare accordingly.

Transportation is another domain within the supply chain that greatly benefits from predictive visibility. By analyzing real-time and historical traffic data, weather reports, and vehicle performance metrics, Python-based models can predict the best routes and schedules for shipments. This not only improves delivery reliability but also contributes to cost-efficiency by reducing fuel consumption and avoiding delays.

The integration of Internet of Things (IoT) devices within the supply chain also plays a pivotal role in predictive visibility. IoT sensors can collect data on various parameters such as temperature, humidity, and location, which Python can process in real time to provide insights into the condition and whereabouts of goods. This data, when fed into predictive models, can alert supply chain managers to potential quality issues or deviations from the expected delivery path, enabling them to act promptly to rectify the situation.

Predictive visibility is not limited to internal operations; it also extends to the customer experience. By analyzing customer data and feedback, Python's machine learning models can predict customer needs and preferences. This allows companies to customize their communication and services, providing updates and offers that are relevant to the individual customer, thereby enhancing satisfaction and loyalty.

The implementation of predictive visibility strategies requires not only technical expertise but also a cultural embrace of data-driven decision-making. Supply chain professionals must be well-versed in the interpretation of analytical models and be able to translate the insights into actionable plans. Continuous learning and adaptation are key, as models need to be regularly refined and updated to reflect the ever-changing dynamics of the supply chain.

Analytics for predictive visibility represents a strategic investment in the future-readiness of supply chain operations. By leveraging Python's analytical prowess, businesses can transform raw data into predictive insights that not only streamline operations but also deliver a more responsive and personalized service to their customers. As the digital landscape evolves, the role of predictive visibility will become increasingly integral to maintaining a resilient and customer-focused supply chain.

CHAPTER 6: SUPPLIER RELATIONSHIP AND RISK MANAGEMENT

Supplier Segmentation and Performance Analysis

The intricate dance of supply chain management is predicated on the partners we choose to engage with — our suppliers. Supplier segmentation and performance analysis are crucial factors in optimizing these relationships, ensuring that the most is made of each partnership. It is a strategic approach that categorizes suppliers based on various criteria, such as risk level, spending, and performance metrics, to tailor the management efforts accordingly.

Segmentation begins with an in-depth analysis of the supplier base, leveraging a range of data points to classify suppliers into meaningful groups. This could involve categorizing suppliers based on their strategic importance, the volume of business they handle, or their compliance with sustainability practices. By dissecting the supplier base into discrete segments, companies can allocate their resources more effectively and foster more targeted relationships.

In segmenting suppliers, companies often turn to the Kraljic Matrix, a model that guides the categorization process by assessing two key dimensions: the risk associated with supply failure and the importance of the purchased items to the company's profitability. This analysis yields four types of suppliers: strategic, bottleneck, leverage, and non-critical. Python's data manipulation libraries, like pandas, facilitate the handling of supplier data and support the application of the Kraljic Matrix through its flexible data structures and rich functionalities for analysis.

Once suppliers are segmented, performance analysis comes into play. This phase involves measuring and monitoring the suppliers against a set of predefined Key Performance Indicators (KPIs). Companies may choose to assess suppliers on criteria such as delivery time, quality of goods, cost management, and innovation contribution. Python's data visualization libraries, such as Matplotlib and Seaborn, allow for the creation of intuitive dashboards and reports that display performance data in an accessible and visually compelling manner.

Performance analysis is not a static exercise. It's dynamic and should be approached as a continuous process. Advanced analytics can be employed to identify trends and patterns in supplier performance over time. By utilizing Python's machine learning libraries, such as scikit-learn, companies can build predictive models to forecast supplier behavior, assess risks, and even to predict the impact of supplier performance on overall supply chain efficiency.

This continuous evaluation feeds back into the segmentation model, as suppliers may shift between categories over time based on their performance and changing business needs. This fluidity necessitates an agile approach to supplier relationship management, where strategies are adapted to reflect the current standing of each supplier segment.

Furthermore, performance analysis can be enriched with sentiment analysis of supplier communication using natural language processing (NLP) techniques available in Python libraries such as NLTK or spaCy. Understanding the sentiment behind supplier communications can provide insights into the health of the relationship, potential frustrations, or areas that require attention.

Effective supplier segmentation and performance analysis lead to a more nuanced understanding of the supplier landscape. It enables supply chain managers to develop bespoke strategies for each segment, whether it's nurturing growth in strategic partnerships, mitigating risks with bottleneck suppliers, driving cost efficiencies with leverage suppliers, or streamlining processes with non-critical suppliers.

In essence, this analytical approach to supplier management not only enhances operational performance but also fosters a collaborative environment where both parties are engaged in the pursuit of mutual growth and success. It is through this lens of strategic segmentation and analysis that supply chains can truly optimize their collaborations, creating a robust network that is both resilient and adaptive to the demands of the modern business ecosystem.

Risk Identification and Assessment Models

Navigating the treacherous waters of supply chain management necessitates a vigilant eye towards potential risks that could capsize the vessel of enterprise. Risk identification and assessment models are instrumental tools in the preemptive detection and evaluation of threats that could disrupt supply chain operations. Akin to a lighthouse in a stormy sea, these models illuminate the path to safety, guiding supply chain managers away from hidden dangers.

The initial step in the risk management process is the identification of risks, which can be intrinsic or extrinsic to the supply chain. Intrinsic risks are those that originate from within the supply chain, such as production bottlenecks or internal failures in quality control. Extrinsic risks, on the other hand, are external forces that impact the supply chain, including economic downturns, natural disasters, or geopolitical tensions.

For comprehensive risk identification, a systematic approach is adopted, often starting with a risk register — a living document that lists all identified risks along with their characteristics. Tools such as Failure Mode and Effects Analysis (FMEA) assist in cataloging potential failures and their effects on the supply chain. Python's robust data-handling capabilities can be harnessed to structure and analyze vast amounts of risk-related data, thus supporting the prioritization of risks based on their likelihood and potential impact.

Following identification, the assessment phase evaluates the significance of each risk. This is where quantitative models, such as Monte Carlo simulations or decision trees, become invaluable. Python, with its powerful libraries like NumPy and SciPy, enables the execution of these complex simulations, providing a probabilistic analysis of risk impact. Such models help in quantifying the uncertainty and assist in decision-making by determining the probability of various risk scenarios.

Another essential model in risk assessment is the Supply Chain Risk Management (SCRM) framework. This multidimensional approach considers various risk categories — operational, financial, strategic, and hazard-related — and evaluates them using a combination of qualitative and quantitative methods. By integrating data analytics and machine learning, the SCRM framework can evolve into a predictive tool, foreseeing potential disruptions with increased accuracy.

A pivotal component of risk assessment is the risk matrix, a tool that visually plots risks according to their severity and likelihood. This facilitates an immediate understanding of which risks require urgent attention. Python's data visualization libraries, like Plotly, can be employed to generate interactive risk matrices that supply chain managers can use to communicate risk profiles to stakeholders clearly.

One must not underestimate the power of machine learning in risk assessment. Predictive models are trained on historical data to recognize patterns that precede disruptive events. Through the use of Python's machine learning libraries, such as TensorFlow and Keras, predictive models can become sophisticated enough to provide early warnings, enabling proactive measures rather than reactive responses.

Risk identification and assessment models, when properly implemented, act as the sentinels of the supply chain, always on guard against the unpredictability of the business environment. They provide a structured approach to risk management, allowing businesses to prepare contingency plans and maintain the resilience of their supply chains against potential disruptions.

In this complex and ever-changing landscape, the judicious

application of these models not only safeguards the operational continuity but also confers a competitive advantage. Companies that can foresee and mitigate risks swiftly can navigate through turbulence with minimal impact, emerging stronger and more adaptable in the face of adversity. This strategic foresight is what distinguishes a resilient supply chain from a vulnerable one, ensuring that the flow of goods and services remains uninterrupted, come what may.

Supplier Collaboration and Innovation

In the intricate tapestry of supply chain networks, supplier collaboration stands out as a pivotal thread that binds various entities into a cohesive fabric of productivity and innovation. The symbiotic relationships that enterprises foster with their suppliers are no longer just transactional engagements; they have evolved into strategic alliances that drive mutual growth and innovation.

Collaboration with suppliers transcends the traditional boundaries of buyer-seller dynamics, venturing into the realms of shared visions and collective problem-solving. It is a proactive approach that encourages open communication, transparency, and joint efforts in developing solutions that benefit all parties involved.

A cornerstone of effective supplier collaboration is the alignment of objectives. Companies and their suppliers must work towards a common goal, finding synergy in their strategies and operations. This alignment is achieved through structured programs such as Vendor Managed Inventory (VMI), where suppliers are given the responsibility to manage the inventory levels of their products at the customer's location. Such programs are underpinned by trust and mutual understanding, leading to reduced stockouts and optimization of inventory costs.

Innovation is another critical aspect of supplier collaboration. Suppliers can be invaluable sources of new ideas, technologies, and processes that can significantly improve product quality, reduce costs, and enhance customer satisfaction. To capitalize on this potential, companies are engaging suppliers early in the product development process, inviting them to contribute their expertise and insights. This co-creation approach can lead to breakthrough innovations that might not have been possible in isolation.

Python plays a significant role in enabling supplier collaboration and innovation. For instance, Python's data analysis libraries, such as Pandas and Matplotlib, can be used to analyze supplier performance data, identify trends and areas for improvement, and share these insights with suppliers in an interactive and engaging manner. This data-driven approach ensures that decisions are based on empirical evidence rather than intuition.

Moreover, machine learning algorithms implemented with Python can help predict supplier-related risks and uncover opportunities for innovation. By analyzing historical data on supplier performance, market trends, and consumer preferences, machine learning models can provide actionable intelligence that supports strategic decision-making.

Another area where Python aids collaboration is in the creation of shared digital platforms. These platforms serve as centralized hubs where companies and suppliers can exchange information, manage contracts, and track the progress of joint initiatives. Python's versatility and its vast ecosystem of web development frameworks, such as Django and Flask, make it an ideal choice for building robust, secure, and scalable digital platforms that facilitate real-time collaboration.

Effective supplier collaboration and innovation also hinge on the adoption of standardized processes and technologies. By employing common tools and platforms, such as Enterprise Resource Planning (ERP) systems integrated with Python-based analytics, companies can ensure that suppliers are working with accurate and up-to-date information. This harmonization reduces errors, streamlines communication, and accelerates the pace of innovation.

The impact of successful supplier collaboration and innovation is profound. It leads to improved supply chain resilience, as partners can quickly adapt to changes and resolve issues collectively. It fosters a culture of continuous improvement, where suppliers are motivated to constantly seek ways to enhance their offerings. Ultimately, it creates a competitive edge for the company, as it can leverage the collective strength of its supplier network to deliver superior value to its customers.

Supplier collaboration and innovation represent a strategic imperative in today's dynamic business environment. By embracing open collaboration and harnessing the power of Python for data analysis and platform development, companies can unlock the full potential of their supplier relationships. This collaborative ethos not only enhances operational efficiency and drives innovation but also solidifies the company's position in the market as a leader capable of delivering exceptional value through its supply chain partnerships.

Sourcing Analytics and Procurement Intelligence

Delving into the world of procurement, sourcing analytics

emerges as a transformative force, redefining the landscape of procurement intelligence with its robust data-driven insights. In the modern supply chain, the ability to make informed, strategic decisions in procurement is not just advantageous; it is imperative for survival and growth.

Sourcing analytics harnesses the vast seas of data available to procurement teams, applying rigorous analysis to uncover patterns, opportunities, and risks. This analytical process involves assessing spend data, supplier performance metrics, market trends, and procurement workflows to illuminate the most cost-effective and efficient paths for sourcing materials and services.

At the heart of sourcing analytics lies the aim to optimize the procurement process. By leveraging advanced analytical tools, procurement professionals can achieve a granular understanding of spending across different categories, departments, and suppliers. This level of detail empowers organizations to negotiate better terms, consolidate purchases for volume discounts, and identify alternative suppliers who can offer better value or innovation.

Python, with its powerful data manipulation libraries such as NumPy and SciPy, enables procurement teams to perform complex calculations and simulations that inform sourcing strategies. For example, Python's capabilities can be applied to conduct what-if analyses, allowing companies to simulate various sourcing scenarios and predict their outcomes based on changes in market conditions, supplier behavior, or internal demand.

One of the key benefits of sourcing analytics is the enhancement of procurement intelligence. This encompasses not only the knowledge of where money is spent but also an understanding of the external factors that could affect supply markets. By integrating Python's machine learning models, procurement teams can anticipate shifts in commodity prices, currency fluctuations, and geopolitical events that may impact sourcing decisions.

Furthermore, Python's machine learning algorithms can assist in supplier segmentation, categorizing suppliers based on various risk factors, performance metrics, and strategic importance. This segmentation enables organizations to prioritize their engagement efforts, focusing on nurturing relationships with critical suppliers while managing risks associated with others.

Sourcing analytics also plays a crucial role in supplier evaluation and selection. By analyzing supplier data, such as quality records, delivery punctuality, and compliance with standards, procurement teams can employ objective, data-based criteria for selecting suppliers. This approach reduces subjectivity in the sourcing process and increases the likelihood of forming successful and lasting partnerships.

In addition to traditional data sources, sourcing analytics can incorporate unstructured data from social media, news outlets, and industry reports using Python's natural language processing (NLP) libraries like NLTK and spaCy. This capability allows procurement teams to gauge market sentiment, monitor brand reputation, and stay abreast of emerging trends that could influence sourcing strategies.

The strategic integration of sourcing analytics into procurement processes leads to a more agile and responsive supply chain. With real-time data and predictive insights, procurement teams can adapt quickly to market changes, ensuring continuity of supply and avoiding costly disruptions. Moreover, the intelligence gleaned from sourcing analytics can be shared across the organization, aligning procurement activities with broader business objectives.

In essence, sourcing analytics and procurement intelligence form a vital nexus in the pursuit of supply chain excellence. Utilizing the computational prowess of Python to dissect and interpret data, organizations can elevate their procurement strategies, making informed decisions that drive cost savings, enhance supplier partnerships, and ultimately contribute to a more resilient and competitive supply chain.

Contract Management and Compliance Analytics

In the intricate web of the supply chain, contract management stands as a critical pillar, ensuring that agreements with suppliers and partners are honored and effectively monitored. Compliance analytics serves as the guardrail, providing the necessary oversight to maintain adherence to contractual obligations and regulatory standards.

The realm of contract management extends beyond the mere execution of agreements; it encompasses the ongoing analysis of contract performance, risk management, and the enforcement of compliance. Organizations that effectively apply analytics to contract management can anticipate potential breaches, enforce compliance proactively, and optimize contract terms to align with evolving business goals and market conditions.

At the core of this function is the meticulous analysis of

contractual data, which includes terms, conditions, pricing structures, and service level agreements (SLAs). This data, when combined with performance metrics and external market intelligence, offers a comprehensive view of the contractual landscape. It enables procurement teams to assess whether suppliers are meeting their obligations, delivering value, and operating within the agreed-upon frameworks.

The utilization of advanced analytics tools in Python, such as Pandas for data manipulation and Matplotlib for data visualization, allows organizations to transform raw contract data into actionable insights. These insights can facilitate the identification of cost-saving opportunities, such as renegotiating contracts that are not in line with current market rates or consolidating contracts to leverage economies of scale.

Compliance analytics, a subset of contract management, employs sophisticated algorithms to monitor and ensure that contractual terms are being adhered to and that regulatory requirements are met. It becomes particularly crucial in industries subject to stringent regulations, such as pharmaceuticals, aerospace, and finance. Python's robust libraries, including scikit-learn for machine learning, can be enlisted to build models that predict compliance risks and flag anomalies in contract execution.

For example, a machine learning model might be trained on historical compliance data to recognize patterns that precede a breach. With this predictive capability, organizations can take preemptive measures to rectify potential issues before they escalate into costly legal disputes or regulatory penalties.

The dynamic nature of compliance, shaped by an ever-changing regulatory environment, demands constant vigilance.

Python's ability to automate the extraction and analysis of regulatory documents, through web scraping libraries like Beautiful Soup, keeps organizations abreast of the latest compliance requirements. This proactive approach to regulatory change management minimizes the risk of non-compliance and ensures that contracts are always aligned with current laws and standards.

Another aspect that falls under the purview of contract management and compliance analytics is the performance of audits. These audits, informed by data analytics, can reveal discrepancies between what is stipulated in contracts and the actual practices being followed. Python's scripting capabilities facilitate the automation of audit processes, allowing for more frequent and thorough reviews that maintain the integrity of the procurement function.

In the event of deviations from agreed-upon terms, compliance analytics provides a mechanism for corrective action. It enables procurement teams to engage in informed discussions with suppliers, armed with evidence-based findings, to swiftly address issues and implement improvements.

Ultimately, contract management and compliance analytics act as the stewards of trust and accountability within the supply chain. By leveraging the data-centric capabilities of Python, organizations gain the visibility needed to manage contracts proactively, uphold compliance, and foster a culture of transparency and performance excellence. As supply chains continue to grow in complexity, the strategic application of analytics in contract management will become increasingly vital, serving as a linchpin for successful supplier relationships and operational efficiency.

Supplier Risk Mitigation Strategies

Navigating the tempestuous waters of the global supply chain necessitates a robust strategy to mitigate risks associated with suppliers. A steadfast approach to supplier risk mitigation not only safeguards a company's operations from disruptions but also fortifies its competitive standing in the marketplace.

Risk mitigation begins with a thorough risk assessment, identifying the multifaceted risks that may arise from a company's supply base. These risks range from financial instability and geopolitical issues to natural disasters and quality failures. To manage these risks effectively, companies must develop a comprehensive strategy that is both reactive, to address immediate issues, and proactive, to prevent future risks.

Python, with its rich ecosystem of data analysis libraries, proves invaluable in quantifying and prioritizing supplier risks. For instance, financial risk can be assessed using Python's NumPy and pandas libraries to analyze suppliers' financial health indicators, such as liquidity ratios or credit scores. Meanwhile, geopolitical risks might be monitored through sentiment analysis of news articles using natural language processing (NLP) libraries like NLTK or spaCy.

Once risks are identified, companies must establish a supplier risk management framework. This involves categorizing suppliers based on their criticality to the business and the magnitude of potential risks they pose. Critical suppliers, for example, may require more intensive monitoring and contingency planning. Python can automate much of this categorization process through clustering algorithms, which can group suppliers based on risk profiles.

After categorizing suppliers, developing a risk mitigation plan is essential. This includes establishing clear communication channels for rapid response, diversifying the supplier base to avoid over-reliance on any single source, and implementing joint risk management programs with key suppliers. Python's SciPy library can assist in modeling different risk scenarios, helping supply chain managers to understand the potential impact of supply disruptions and to simulate the effects of various mitigation strategies.

Contractual safeguards are another cornerstone of risk mitigation. Companies should negotiate contracts that include clauses for performance guarantees, penalties for non-compliance, and stipulations for transparency. Analytics can play a role here, as well, by tracking supplier performance against contractual agreements. Python's matplotlib library can visualize this performance data, making it easier to identify trends and outliers that may indicate emerging risks.

Supply chain managers also need to regularly review and update their risk mitigation strategies to adapt to the ever-changing risk landscape. This is where machine learning models come into play, as they can be trained and retrained on new data to forecast potential risks more accurately. In Python, machine learning models can be implemented using libraries like scikit-learn, which offers a range of supervised and unsupervised learning algorithms.

Scenario planning, backed by Python's robust simulation capabilities, enables managers to explore the outcomes of different risk mitigation strategies under various future states of the world. Libraries such as SimPy allow for the creation of complex simulations that model the interdependencies within the supply chain and the ripple effects of potential disruptions.

Supplier risk mitigation strategies are a critical component of a resilient supply chain. By leveraging Python's powerful data analysis and machine learning tools, companies can gain a deeper understanding of the risks they face, develop informed mitigation strategies, and react swiftly to changing conditions. The goal is not just to respond to risks as they occur but to anticipate and prevent them, ensuring a smooth and uninterrupted flow of goods and services across the global supply chain.

Impact of Geopolitical Factors on Supplier Risk

The intricate tapestry of global supply chains is vulnerable to the whims of geopolitical dynamics, which can introduce substantial risks to supplier relationships. The impact of such factors is profound, often triggering cascading effects that ripple through supply networks with surprising speed and force.

In the realm of supplier risk management, geopolitical factors include, but are not limited to, trade policies, economic sanctions, regional conflicts, and political instability. These elements can lead to sudden changes in the cost of goods, the availability of raw materials, and can even sever supply lines overnight. Thus, comprehending and mitigating the risks posed by geopolitical forces is not just prudent; it's imperative for the longevity and resilience of supply chains.

To illustrate, consider the imposition of tariffs on imported goods. Such a policy shift can instantly transform a supplier's competitive pricing into a financial burden. Using Python, analysts can simulate the financial impact of tariffs on the supply chain. By applying libraries such as pandas for data manipulation and NumPy for numerical calculations, analysts can model various tariff scenarios and their potential effects on costs.

Political instability, another geopolitical factor, can disrupt supply chains by causing delays or cessation of production. In regions where this risk is significant, supply chain managers can employ Python's geospatial libraries, like GeoPandas, to map supplier locations against political risk indices, thus visualizing high-risk zones and enabling preemptive action.

Economic sanctions present a different kind of challenge. A supplier located in a sanctioned country may suddenly become off-limits, necessitating rapid sourcing alternatives. Data analysis tools in Python can help identify and assess the viability of alternative suppliers in real-time, allowing companies to pivot quickly and minimize disruption.

Furthermore, regional conflicts can not only disrupt but also endanger the supply chain. Understanding the nature of these conflicts and their potential to affect suppliers is a complex task that involves analyzing large volumes of data. Here, Python's machine learning capabilities, through libraries like scikit-learn, can uncover patterns and predict the escalation of regional tensions, providing a valuable window for proactive measures.

It is crucial to monitor these geopolitical factors continuously, as they can evolve swiftly and unpredictably. Advanced analytics, particularly predictive analytics, can process vast arrays of political, economic, and social data to forecast potential disruptions. By integrating APIs from reputable geopolitical risk assessment providers into Python scripts, companies can automate the collection and analysis of up-to-date intelligence, thereby maintaining a vigilant stance against geopolitical risks.

In managing these risks, diversification of suppliers emerges as a strategic imperative. By leveraging optimization algorithms in Python, such as those found in the SciPy library, supply chain managers can design a diversified supplier network that minimizes reliance on any one geopolitical area.

Lastly, the importance of agility in responding to geopolitical changes cannot be overstated. An agile supply chain can adapt its sourcing strategies, production locations, and logistics plans on the fly in response to geopolitical shifts. Python's robust data processing and simulation capabilities enable the rapid reconfiguration of supply chain networks, ensuring businesses can navigate the geopolitical landscape with confidence and resilience.

In summary, the impact of geopolitical factors on supplier risk is a critical consideration for supply chain managers. By utilizing the power of Python and its vast ecosystem of libraries, businesses can gain insights into geopolitical risks, model their potential impacts, and develop agile strategies to mitigate these risks. This approach positions companies to not only weather the storms of geopolitical upheaval but to emerge from them more robust and adaptable than ever.

Resilience and Agility in Supplier Management

In the pursuit of a robust supply chain, resilience and agility stand as twin pillars, enabling organizations to withstand disruptions and adapt to changes with rapidity and finesse. Supplier management is at the heart of these efforts, serving as a critical leverage point for enhancing overall supply chain performance.

Resilience in supplier management is about building the capacity to recover quickly from difficulties. It is not just about having backup plans but also about having suppliers that can withstand various types of shocks, whether they be natural disasters, economic downturns, or technological failures. To build resilience, companies must engage in thorough risk assessments, evaluating suppliers' operational, financial, and reputational stability. In doing so, they must consider the entire ecosystem in which the suppliers operate, including the political, socio-economic, and environmental contexts.

Agility, on the other hand, is about the speed and flexibility with which a supply chain can respond to change. Agile supplier management practices allow companies to respond to short-term variations in demand or supply without compromising long-term strategic goals. This includes having the ability to switch suppliers, alter production quantities, or reroute supply chains when necessary.

In practical terms, resilience might involve diversifying the supplier base to avoid over-reliance on any single source or geographic location. It also means building strong relationships with suppliers, fostering open communication channels, and collaborating on contingency planning. For example, a Python-based supply chain simulation might run scenarios where certain suppliers are suddenly unavailable; the outcomes would guide the development of robust contingency plans.

Agility could be reflected in contractual arrangements that allow for flexible order quantities or delivery timings, in response to market fluctuations. It also involves implementing advanced technologies such as cloud-based platforms for real-time collaboration with suppliers.

For instance, consider a scenario where a sudden spike in demand requires rapid scaling of production. Python can be used to quickly analyze which suppliers have the capacity to meet this demand. Using Python's data visualization libraries like Matplotlib or Seaborn, supply chain managers can create dashboards that display suppliers' performance metrics, enabling faster decision-making.

Moreover, machine learning models can predict supplier performance based on historical data, allowing for preemptive actions to be taken in case of potential issues. For example, a predictive model might highlight a supplier's likelihood to deliver late, prompting the supply chain manager to allocate additional buffer stock or identify alternative suppliers in advance.

Technological solutions such as IoT devices can provide real-time data on a supplier's manufacturing processes, inventory levels, and shipment status. This data can be streamed into Python-based analytics systems for ongoing monitoring and rapid analysis, enabling quicker responses to emerging situations.

In the realm of supplier management, agility also means being able to innovate alongside suppliers. This might involve co-developing new products, adopting joint practices for sustainability, or sharing knowledge and resources to overcome mutual challenges. Through such partnerships, the entire supply chain becomes more responsive and capable of navigating the complexities of the modern business landscape.

In conclusion, resilience and agility in supplier management are not merely buzzwords but essential strategies for supply chain excellence. They demand a proactive approach to risk management, continuous improvement, and the use of sophisticated analytical tools and technologies. By embedding these qualities into the fabric of supplier management, organizations can create supply chains that are not just efficient and cost-effective but also robust enough to thrive in an ever-changing global market.

Predictive Analytics for Supplier Risk

The implementation of predictive analytics in supplier risk management is a transformative approach that serves as a crystal ball, offering foresight into potential supply chain disruptions before they crystallize into crises. By harnessing historical data and machine learning algorithms, organizations gain the ability to anticipate and mitigate risks associated with their suppliers.

Predictive analytics revolves around the use of statistical models and forecasting algorithms to analyze patterns and trends within large datasets. In the context of supplier risk management, this means evaluating numerous variables that might affect a supplier's performance, including geopolitical events, currency fluctuations, market trends, and even weather patterns.

```python
import pandas as pd
from sklearn.model_selection import train_test_split
from sklearn.ensemble import RandomForestClassifier

# Load the supplier data
supplier_data = pd.read_csv('supplier_risk_data.csv')
```

```
# Preprocess the data (e.g., handling missing values, encoding
categorical variables)
supplier_data_preprocessed = preprocess_data(supplier_data)

# Split the dataset into training and test sets
X_train, X_test, y_train, y_test = train_test_split(
    random_state=42
)

# Initialize the Random Forest Classifier
rf_classifier   =   RandomForestClassifier(n_estimators=100,
random_state=42)

# Train the model on the training data
rf_classifier.fit(X_train, y_train)

# Predict risk levels on the test set
risk_predictions = rf_classifier.predict(X_test)
```
```

Here, a RandomForestClassifier is used to predict the risk level of suppliers based on historical data. This is a simplified example, but it embodies the essence of how predictive analytics can inform risk management decisions.

Once predictive models are in place, they can be used to generate risk scores for each supplier, identifying which ones might be prone to disruptions. These risk scores enable supply chain managers to proactively engage with high-risk suppliers to discuss risk mitigation strategies or to diversify their supplier
```

base accordingly.

Predictive analytics can also facilitate what-if analysis, allowing managers to simulate the impact of potential risks and their propagation through the supply chain. Python's simulation libraries, such as SimPy, can model the supply chain as a system and simulate the ripple effects of supplier failures.

Furthermore, predictive analytics extends beyond identifying risks. It can also highlight opportunities for supply chain optimization. For example, machine learning can uncover patterns indicating when a supplier is likely to offer discounts or when the quality of materials is at its peak, thus enabling strategic purchasing decisions.

In embracing predictive analytics for supplier risk management, organizations adopt a proactive stance, replacing reactive fire-fighting with strategic risk avoidance. This transition to a data-driven approach not only strengthens the resilience of supply chains but also offers competitive advantage, as it allows companies to navigate uncertainties with greater confidence and strategic insight.

The integration of predictive analytics into supplier risk management represents a paradigm shift from traditional, reactive approaches to a forward-looking, data-empowered strategy. By leveraging Python and advanced analytics, businesses can illuminate the path ahead, ensuring their supply chain remains robust against the unpredictable tides of the global marketplace.

Ethical and Responsible Sourcing

In the intricate web of modern supply chains, ethical and

responsible sourcing has ascended as a beacon of corporate integrity and sustainability. This paradigm advocates for sourcing practices that are not only economically sound but also socially and environmentally conscientious. Ethical sourcing prioritizes the welfare of all stakeholders, from the laborers in the supply chain to the end consumers, and extends to the stewardship of our planet's resources.

At the heart of ethical and responsible sourcing lies the commitment to transparency and traceability. Businesses must know where their products come from, under what conditions they were produced, and the impact their creation has had on both communities and the environment. This information is pivotal in making informed decisions that align with a company's values and the expectations of its customers.

```python
import matplotlib.pyplot as plt
import pandas as pd

# Load the audit data
audit_data = pd.read_csv('supplier_audit_results.csv')

# Aggregate data by compliance category
compliance_summary = audit_data.groupby('Compliance_Category')['Score'].mean().reset_index()

# Create a bar chart to visualize average scores by category
plt.bar(compliance_summary['Compliance_Category'], compliance_summary['Score'])
```

```
plt.xlabel('Compliance Category')
plt.ylabel('Average Score')
plt.title('Supplier Compliance Score Summary')
plt.show()
```
` ` `

With such visual aids, companies can prioritize interventions and work collaboratively with suppliers to enhance compliance and ethical standards.

Another cornerstone of responsible sourcing is the investment in local communities. By supporting local suppliers and encouraging fair trade practices, businesses can foster economic growth and stability in the regions from which they source. This, in turn, can lead to more resilient and loyal supply bases.

Responsible sourcing also entails a commitment to environmental sustainability. Companies must evaluate the ecological footprint of their sourcing decisions, considering factors such as carbon emissions, water usage, and waste generation. Life cycle assessment (LCA) tools can quantify the environmental impact of products from cradle to grave, guiding companies towards more sustainable choices.

Moreover, ethical sourcing is increasingly becoming a collaborative effort. Blockchain technology, for instance, offers a decentralized and tamper-proof ledger that can track the provenance of goods and ensure the integrity of supply chain data. This enhances the trust between consumers and businesses, ensuring that claims of ethical sourcing are verifiable and not merely marketing rhetoric.

In the digital age, consumer awareness and activism have risen sharply, and with it, the demand for ethically sourced products. Social media and online platforms have given consumers the power to hold companies accountable for their supply chain practices. Consequently, organizations that proactively adopt ethical sourcing strategies not only mitigate risks but also build brand loyalty and competitive differentiation.

In essence, ethical and responsible sourcing is not just a moral imperative but a strategic necessity in the quest for long-term business sustainability. It requires a multifaceted approach, integrating rigorous standards, community investment, environmental stewardship, and technological innovation. By embedding ethical principles into their sourcing strategies, companies can not only ensure compliance but also drive positive change, reinforcing their brand's reputation and securing its place in a conscientious market.

CHAPTER 7:
LEAN AND AGILE
SUPPLY CHAINS

*Principles of Lean Supply
Chain Management*

L ean Supply Chain Management (LSCM) is a philosophy that emphasizes the elimination of waste in all forms within the supply chain, streamlining processes to create value for the end customer with the least amount of resources possible. It is a strategic approach that requires a holistic view of the supply chain to identify non-value-adding activities and systematically remove them. The principles of LSCM are derived from the Lean manufacturing methodologies that were pioneered by Toyota and are characterized by several core tenets.

Value Identification: The first principle is to define what constitutes value from the perspective of the customer. Understanding customer value is paramount as it sets the foundation for all subsequent lean supply chain activities. Once this value is identified, the entire supply chain can be aligned to ensure that every step contributes towards delivering that value.

```python
import pandas as pd
import numpy as np

# Load the process data
process_data = pd.read_csv('supply_chain_processes.csv')

# Identify value-adding processes
value_adding_processes                                          =
process_data[process_data['Value_Adding'] == 'Yes']

# Calculate the time spent on value-adding processes
value_adding_time                                               =
np.sum(value_adding_processes['Process_Time'])

print(f"Total    Time    on    Value-Adding    Processes:
{value_adding_time}")
```

Flow: The third principle is to ensure that the product or service flows smoothly through the supply chain without interruptions, delays, or bottlenecks. Creating a continuous flow improves lead times, reduces inventory levels, and enhances the overall responsiveness of the supply chain.

Pull Systems: Instead of traditional push systems where products are produced in anticipation of demand, lean supply chains operate on pull systems. This principle is about producing only what is needed when it is needed, based on actual customer demand. The use of pull systems is exemplified by Just-In-Time (JIT) delivery, which aims to receive goods only as they are required in the production process, thereby reducing inventory costs.

Perfection: The pursuit of perfection is a relentless quest in a lean supply chain. It involves continuous improvement (Kaizen) through the regular analysis of operations and striving for incremental enhancements in every aspect of the supply chain. Perfection in this context means a commitment to never being satisfied with the status quo and always looking for ways to reduce waste and improve efficiency.

Respect for People: A fundamental principle often overlooked is the respect for people involved in the supply chain. Lean principles are not just about processes but also about empowering employees, encouraging their participation in problem-solving, and respecting their contributions. A supply chain that values its workforce fosters a culture of continuous improvement and innovation.

Responsiveness to Change: Lean supply chains must be adaptable and responsive to changes in customer demand, market conditions, and technological advancements. Agility within a lean framework allows organizations to pivot quickly and efficiently when faced with new challenges or opportunities.

In conclusion, the principles of Lean Supply Chain Management provide a framework for organizations to deliver the highest value to their customers with minimal waste. Implementing these principles requires a deep understanding of customer needs, a commitment to scrutinizing and refining processes, and an organizational culture that embraces change and continuous improvement. Through the application of LSCM, companies can achieve a competitive advantage by becoming more efficient, responsive, and customer-focused.

As the narrative continues to unfold, the principles of lean supply chain management serve as a compass, guiding businesses towards a horizon of operational excellence and sustainable value creation.

Applying Agile Methodologies in the Supply Chain

Agile methodologies, originally conceived for software development, have been successfully adapted to the supply chain sector, offering enhanced flexibility, adaptability, and responsiveness. Applying Agile in the supply chain context involves a distinct shift from traditional planning approaches to a more dynamic, iterative process that can rapidly respond to changing market demands and conditions.

Agile Supply Chain Framework: At the heart of Agile supply chain management is the Agile Supply Chain Framework, which consists of several key components including visibility, adaptability, alignment, and collaboration.

- **Visibility** entails having real-time data at every stage of the supply chain, from supplier inventory levels to customer demand signals. This transparency is crucial for making informed decisions quickly.

- **Adaptability** refers to the capacity of the supply chain to change directions efficiently and effectively, with minimal disruption, in response to external stimuli such as market trends or supply shocks.

- **Alignment** ensures that all elements of the supply chain, including partners and suppliers, are working towards a common set of goals and responding cohesively to changes.

- **Collaboration** is critical in an Agile supply chain as it relies on strong relationships and open communication channels between all parties involved, from suppliers to end customers.

Scrum in Supply Chain Management: One Agile methodology that has been adapted for supply chain management is Scrum. Scrum is an iterative and incremental framework that supports teams in working collaboratively to deliver projects in a more flexible manner. In a supply chain context, Scrum can be used to manage complex logistics projects, with sprints focused on specific deliverables such as the launch of a new distribution center or the integration of a new supplier.

```python
from datetime import datetime, timedelta

# Define the sprint start and end dates
sprint_start = datetime.now()
sprint_end = sprint_start + timedelta(days=14)   # A typical sprint is two weeks

# List of tasks for the sprint
tasks = [
]

# Function to update task status
```

```
        task['status'] = new_status
        return f"Task '{task_name}' status updated to
'{new_status}'."
    return "Task not found."

# Example of updating a task status
print(update_task_status("Optimize    distribution    routes",
"in_progress"))
` ` `
```

To measure the success of Agile adoption in the supply chain, specific KPIs and metrics can be established. These may include lead time, response time to customer inquiries, inventory turnover rates, and the frequency of stockouts. By tracking these metrics over time, supply chain managers can assess the impact of Agile methodologies on overall performance.

Culture plays a significant role in the successful implementation of Agile methodologies. An Agile supply chain culture is characterized by openness to change, a willingness to experiment, and an emphasis on team empowerment. Leadership within such organizations must foster an environment that encourages creativity, learning from failures, and celebrating iterative improvements.

While the benefits of Agile in the supply chain are numerous, there are challenges to its implementation. Organizations often face resistance to change, particularly from those accustomed to traditional, plan-driven approaches. Additionally, the lack of standardization in Agile practices can lead to confusion and inconsistency if not managed properly.

In conclusion, applying Agile methodologies to the supply chain empowers organizations to navigate the complexities of today's fast-paced business environment. With its focus on flexibility, continuous improvement, and customer satisfaction, Agile supply chain management is a potent strategy for companies looking to enhance their operational resilience and competitive edge. Moving forward, the narrative will explore how organizations can further integrate Agile practices into their operations, ensuring that they remain at the forefront of supply chain innovation.

Six Sigma in Supply Chain Analytics

The Six Sigma methodology, with its roots in manufacturing, is a data-driven approach designed to improve processes by eliminating defects and reducing variability. Its principles and tools are readily applicable to supply chain analytics, enhancing the reliability and efficiency of supply chain operations.

Six Sigma's DMAIC Framework in Supply Chain: The DMAIC (Define, Measure, Analyze, Improve, Control) framework is the cornerstone of Six Sigma and serves as a systematic method for process improvement within the supply chain.

- **Define**: The initial phase involves defining the problem or the process that needs improvement within the supply chain. This could involve delivery delays, high defect rates in products, or inventory management issues.

- **Measure**: The next step is to quantitatively measure the current performance of the process. This could involve collecting data on delivery times, defect rates, or inventory levels using various data collection methods.

- **Analyze**: With data in hand, the analysis phase seeks to identify the root causes of the process inefficiencies. Advanced analytics and data mining techniques can reveal patterns and correlations that were not immediately obvious.

- **Improve**: Based on the analysis, solutions are proposed and implemented to improve the process. This could involve redesigning the supply chain network, implementing quality control measures, or optimizing inventory levels.

- **Control**: The final phase ensures that the improvements are sustained over time. This may involve establishing monitoring systems, creating control charts, and training staff to follow the new procedures.

Applying Six Sigma Tools: Various tools are available within the Six Sigma toolkit that can be particularly useful in supply chain analytics. For example, a Pareto chart can help identify the most common causes of shipping delays, while a process map can uncover inefficiencies in the order-to-delivery cycle.

```python
import matplotlib.pyplot as plt
import pandas as pd

# Sample data: types of defects and their frequencies
defect_data = {
    'Frequency': [150, 75, 300, 50]
}

# Create a DataFrame
df = pd.DataFrame(defect_data)
```

```
# Sort the defects by frequency in descending order
df_sorted = df.sort_values(by='Frequency', ascending=False)

# Calculate the cumulative percentage
df_sorted['Cumulative Percentage'] = df_sorted['Frequency'].cumsum() / df_sorted['Frequency'].sum() * 100

# Create a Pareto chart
fig, ax = plt.subplots()
df_sorted['Frequency'].plot(kind='bar', color='blue', ax=ax)
df_sorted['Cumulative Percentage'].plot(kind='line', marker='o', secondary_y=True, ax=ax)

ax.set_title('Pareto Chart of Supply Chain Defects')
ax.set_xlabel('Defect Type')
ax.set_ylabel('Frequency')

# Show the chart
plt.show()
```

Integrating Six Sigma in Supply Chain Culture: To fully realize the benefits of Six Sigma in supply chain analytics, it must be woven into the organizational fabric. This integration demands a commitment from top management and a willingness at all levels of the organization to embrace data-driven decision-making and continuous improvement.

Challenges of Implementing Six Sigma: The path to integrating

Six Sigma into the supply chain is not without its challenges. It requires a significant investment in training and upskilling employees to use Six Sigma tools effectively. Moreover, a culture shift towards embracing data and analytics can sometimes be slow to take hold in organizations entrenched in traditional ways of working.

In essence, Six Sigma in supply chain analytics offers a structured approach to problem-solving that can lead to substantial improvements in efficiency, cost savings, and customer satisfaction. By applying Six Sigma's rigorous data analysis and process improvement techniques, supply chain managers can markedly enhance their operations' performance, thereby gaining an edge in an increasingly competitive marketplace.

Just-In-Time (JIT) and Kanban Systems

At the intersection of efficiency and responsiveness in supply chain management lies the Just-In-Time (JIT) methodology. JIT, a philosophy with Japanese origins, is predicated on the timely production and delivery of goods, not just in time for sale, but precisely when they are needed, thereby reducing waste and inventory costs. When JIT is harmonized with Kanban systems, a visual workflow management tool, they become formidable instruments for achieving lean supply chain operations.

Essence of JIT: JIT focuses on the continuous alignment of production processes with customer demands. The main objective is to produce the right amount, at the right time, and in the right place, thus minimizing waste across the supply chain. Inventory is seen not as an asset but a liability, and by reducing it, companies can unleash capital that can be invested elsewhere.

Kanban System Integration: Kanban, which translates to "visual signal" or "card" in Japanese, complements JIT by providing a visual system to manage work and inventory at each stage of the production process. In a Kanban system, a card or a digital marker signals when a new batch of production should start or when more materials need to be ordered.

```python
# A simple text-based Kanban board in Python
from collections import defaultdict

# Define a class for the Kanban board
        self.columns = defaultdict(list)

        self.columns[column].append(task)

        print(f"{column}:")
            print(f" - {task}")
        print()

# Initialize Kanban board with three columns
kanban = KanbanBoard()

# Adding tasks to the Kanban board
kanban.add_task('To Do', 'Order raw materials')
kanban.add_task('In Progress', 'Manufacture part A')
kanban.add_task('Done', 'Assemble product X')

# Displaying the Kanban board
```

```
kanban.display_board()
` ` `
```

JIT's Impact on Supply Chains: JIT can significantly reduce costs and improve product quality. By synchronizing production schedules closely with demand forecasts and customer orders, companies can avoid the expense of storing large amounts of inventory and reduce the risk of obsolescence.

Kanban for JIT Efficiency: Kanban signals help maintain the smooth flow of resources through the production process, which is essential for JIT implementation. It ensures that workstations only produce what is needed downstream, thus preventing overproduction—one of the key wastes in lean methodology.

Challenges of JIT and Kanban Implementation: While the benefits of JIT and Kanban systems are compelling, their implementation can be challenging. It requires a deep understanding of the production process, the ability to predict and adapt to changes in demand accurately, and a highly responsive supply chain network. Any disruptions in the supply chain, such as supplier delays or transportation issues, can lead to production halts, as there is little inventory to fall back on.

Furthermore, JIT and Kanban require a cultural shift within the organization, where all employees must understand the importance of their role in the process and be committed to continuous improvement and waste elimination.

By leveraging the strengths of JIT and Kanban systems, organizations can create a more agile and cost-effective supply chain. The key lies in meticulous planning, a collaborative culture, and a resilient supply network that can adapt to the dynamic nature of demand, all of which can be fostered and enhanced through the strategic application of supply chain analytics.

Value Stream Mapping and Process Flow Analysis

In the realm of lean supply chain management, Value Stream Mapping (VSM) is an invaluable tool for dissecting and understanding the flow of materials and information as they make their journey from supplier to customer. Coupled with rigorous process flow analysis, VSM is instrumental in identifying bottlenecks, eliminating waste, and optimizing the overall value chain for efficiency and effectiveness.

Delving into VSM: Value Stream Mapping is a visual means to represent every step of a product's lifecycle - from raw material sourcing to the end customer - and the information flows that enable this journey. By mapping out all these activities, organizations gain a bird's-eye view of the entire process, making it easier to pinpoint inefficiencies and areas ripe for improvement.

Process Flow Analysis for Streamlining: Process flow analysis goes hand-in-hand with VSM, providing a granular look at each stage of the value stream. It involves the examination of each process step, considering factors such as time, cost, and resource utilization, to ensure that each process is adding value rather than contributing to waste.

```python
# A simple Python script for analyzing process times in a value stream

import pandas as pd
```

```
# Sample data representing different process steps and their
times
    'Time (minutes)': [30, 15, 120, 45, 20, 30, 60]}

# Convert the data into a DataFrame
process_data = pd.DataFrame(data)

# Calculate the total time taken for the value stream
total_time = process_data['Time (minutes)'].sum()
print(f"The total time of the value stream is: {total_time}
minutes")

# Identify the longest process step
longest_step       =       process_data.loc[process_data['Time
(minutes)'].idxmax()]
print(f"The longest process step is: {longest_step['Process Step']}
taking {longest_step['Time (minutes)']} minutes")

# Output the process steps in order of time taken, descending
sorted_data = process_data.sort_values(by='Time (minutes)',
ascending=False)
print("\nProcess steps sorted by time (longest to shortest):")
print(sorted_data)
```
```

**Applying VSM and Process Flow Analysis**: When an organization applies VSM and process flow analysis, it commits to a systematic approach for continuous improvement. By highlighting the steps that do not add value - such as wait times, unnecessary movements, or excessive inventory - leaders can
```

make informed decisions to streamline operations.

Cultural Shift for VSM Adoption: Like JIT and Kanban, the adoption of VSM and process flow analysis requires a cultural shift towards a mindset of ongoing improvement. Every employee, from the shop floor to the executive suite, must be engaged in the process and empowered to suggest changes that can lead to a more lean and responsive supply chain.

Enhancing Lean Practices with Analytics: Supply chain analytics can augment VSM and process flow analysis by providing data-driven insights into the value stream. Analytics tools can process large volumes of data quickly, identifying patterns and predicting the impacts of proposed changes before they are implemented. This predictive capability allows for more accurate and strategic decision-making in the pursuit of lean supply chain operations.

The integration of VSM and process flow analysis into the supply chain is not a one-time project but an iterative process. As market conditions and technologies evolve, so too must the value stream. By regularly revisiting and refining the value stream map and process flows, organizations can maintain a competitive edge in an ever-changing business landscape.

Balancing Lean and Responsiveness

The pursuit of a lean supply chain is often seen as the holy grail of operational efficiency. Yet, the relentless drive for leanness must be tempered with the ability to respond swiftly to changing market demands. Achieving the right balance between lean principles and responsiveness is crucial for a supply chain to maintain both cost-effectiveness and customer satisfaction.

The Lean Approach: Lean supply chain management focuses on minimizing waste—be it in the form of excess inventory, unnecessary steps, or time delays—while maximizing value to the customer. It emphasizes a streamlined approach that can often lead to reduced costs and increased efficiency.

Responsiveness in Supply Chain: On the other side of the spectrum, a responsive supply chain is designed to be flexible and adaptable. It can quickly adjust to new trends, fluctuating customer demands, and unexpected disruptions. Responsiveness is about agility, the ability to pivot and react with speed.

Striking the Balance: The crux of modern supply chain strategy lies in finding synergy between lean and responsive practices. On one hand, inventory levels should be kept low; on the other hand, a certain buffer must be maintained to absorb fluctuations in demand. Similarly, while standardized processes are essential for lean operations, there must be room for flexibility to customize products and accommodate special orders.

```python
# A Python script to simulate inventory levels and lead time to
balance lean and responsiveness

import numpy as np
import matplotlib.pyplot as plt

# Define parameters for the simulation
average_demand_per_day = 100
std_dev_demand = 20
```

```
lead_time_days = 10
safety_stock_multiplier = 1.65  # Corresponds to a 95% service
level

# Simulate 30 days of demand
daily_demand = np.random.normal(average_demand_per_day,
std_dev_demand, 30)

# Calculate reorder point to balance lean and responsiveness
reorder_point = average_demand_per_day * lead_time_days
+    (safety_stock_multiplier    *    std_dev_demand    *
np.sqrt(lead_time_days))
inventory_level = reorder_point # Starting inventory level

# Run the simulation
inventory_levels = []
orders_placed = []
    # Place order to replenish inventory
    inventory_level    +=    average_demand_per_day    *
lead_time_days
    orders_placed.append(day)
  # Simulate daily demand
  inventory_level -= daily_demand[day]
  inventory_levels.append(inventory_level)

# Plot the results
plt.figure(figsize=(14, 7))
plt.plot(inventory_levels, label='Inventory Level')
plt.axhline(y=reorder_point,    color='r',    linestyle='--',
```

```
label='Reorder Point')
plt.title('Inventory Level Simulation')
plt.xlabel('Day')
plt.ylabel('Inventory Level')
plt.legend()
plt.grid(True)
plt.show()
```

Leveraging Data for Decision-Making: Data analytics plays a vital role in achieving the balance between lean and responsiveness. By analyzing sales history, market trends, and customer feedback, companies can predict demand more accurately and plan their inventory levels accordingly. Machine learning models can further refine these predictions by learning from a multitude of variables and identifying complex patterns.

Resilience through Flexibility: A balanced supply chain is also a resilient one. By incorporating principles of both lean and responsive supply chains, companies are better equipped to handle disruptions. This resilience is particularly important in an era where supply chains face a wide array of challenges, from natural disasters to trade tensions.

Continuous Improvement and Adaptation: The balance between lean and responsiveness is not static; it must be continually reassessed and adjusted as conditions change. Continuous improvement methodologies such as Kaizen can be employed to regularly refine operations, ensuring that the supply chain remains both efficient and agile.

The fusion of lean and responsive strategies requires a deep understanding of the supply chain, a sophisticated approach to data analytics, and the flexibility to adapt strategies as needed. With these elements in place, companies can enjoy the cost benefits of a lean approach while still meeting the expectations of their customers in a timely manner.

Quick Response and Fast Fashion Supply Chains

In an era where consumer trends can shift in the blink of an eye, quick response (QR) has become an essential strategy, particularly within the realm of fast fashion supply chains. Fast fashion retailers are faced with the dual challenge of constantly refreshing their product offerings while also ensuring that these goods are available to consumers almost as quickly as trends emerge.

Quick Response Explained: Quick response is a management strategy focused on reducing lead times across the supply chain. It involves streamlining the design, production, and distribution processes to accelerate product availability. QR leverages information technology and logistical flexibility to respond rapidly to consumer demands.

Fast Fashion Dynamics: Fast fashion is characterized by rapid production and a high turnover of small-batch collections that mimic current luxury fashion trends. This business model thrives on the ability to quickly move designs from catwalk to store shelves. Speed is of the essence, and QR is the linchpin that enables this velocity.

Implementing QR in Fast Fashion: A critical aspect of QR in fast fashion is the symbiotic relationship between retailers and suppliers. It requires a tightly integrated supply chain where communication flows seamlessly, and production can be ramped up or adjusted at a moment's notice. This includes close collaboration with manufacturers, often through advanced information systems that allow for real-time data exchange.

```python
# A Python script to analyze lead times and identify
opportunities for reduction in a fast fashion supply chain

import pandas as pd

# Sample data representing lead times in days from different
suppliers
data = {
    'Distribution_to_Retail': [2, 3, 2, 1]
}

# Convert the data into a DataFrame
lead_times = pd.DataFrame(data)

# Calculate total lead time for each supplier
lead_times['Total_Lead_Time'] = lead_times.sum(axis=1)

# Identify the supplier with the shortest lead time
min_lead_time_supplier = lead_times.loc[lead_times['Total_Lead_Time'].idxmin()]

print(f"Supplier with shortest total lead time: {min_lead_time_supplier['Supplier']}")
print(f"Total lead time: {min_lead_time_supplier['Total_Lead_Time']} days")
```

```
# Output potential lead time reduction opportunities
print("\nOpportunities for lead time reduction:")
    print(f"- Supplier {row['Supplier']} can reduce design
to production time by {row['Design_to_Production'] -
min_lead_time_supplier['Design_to_Production']} days.")
    print(f"- Supplier {row['Supplier']} can reduce production
to distribution time by {row['Production_to_Distribution'] -
min_lead_time_supplier['Production_to_Distribution']} days.")
    print(f"- Supplier {row['Supplier']} can reduce
distribution to retail time by {row['Distribution_to_Retail'] -
min_lead_time_supplier['Distribution_to_Retail']} days.")
```

Benefits and Drawbacks: The QR approach in fast fashion offers the advantage of a highly reactive supply chain, capable of adapting to trends and consumer preferences quickly. However, it also presents challenges, such as the potential for overproduction and increased waste, ethical concerns regarding labor practices, and the environmental impact of rapid production cycles.

Sustainability Considerations: As the conversation around sustainability grows louder, fast fashion brands are seeking ways to integrate more responsible practices while maintaining the speed that defines them. This includes exploring sustainable materials, investing in recycling initiatives, and adjusting production models to reduce waste.

Adaptive Analytics for Responsive Decisions: Data analytics supports QR by providing actionable insights into consumer behavior, sales patterns, and inventory levels. Predictive analytics can forecast demand surges, allowing for proactive inventory management. Additionally, sentiment analysis tools can scan social media and internet sources to gauge fashion trends as they emerge, further informing production decisions.

The Future of QR: Technological advancements continue to refine QR capabilities. From AI-driven trend prediction to automated production lines, the potential for even faster turnaround times is on the horizon. However, as QR evolves, so must the consideration for its broader implications, balancing the need for speed against the imperative for ethical and sustainable practices.

In conclusion, QR is a defining feature of fast fashion, enabling brands to meet the consumer's appetite for the latest styles without significant lag. By leveraging advanced data analytics and fostering strong supplier relationships, these supply chains can not only be swift but also smarter and more attuned to the shifting landscape of retail and consumer expectations.

Agile Project Management Tools for Supply Chains

Agile project management has revolutionized the way supply chains operate, offering a flexible and iterative approach to managing projects. This adaptability is particularly valuable in the dynamic environment of supply chains, where variables and conditions can change rapidly and unpredictably.

Agile Methodology in Supply Chains: At its core, Agile project management is about embracing change, even late in the development process. It prioritizes customer feedback and continuous improvement, making it well-suited for supply chain projects where customer demand and market conditions are in constant flux.

Tools for Agility: To implement Agile methodologies, supply chain managers leverage various tools designed to support flexibility, collaboration, and visibility. These range from simple kanban boards for visualizing workflow to sophisticated software platforms that facilitate project tracking, resource allocation, and real-time communication among team members.

```python
# A Python script to create a simple kanban board for managing supply chain projects

from collections import defaultdict

# Sample data representing tasks in different stages
tasks = {
    'Done': ['Update procurement policies', 'Conduct market analysis for expansion']
}

# Function to display the kanban board
    kanban_board = defaultdict(list)

        print(f"{stage}:")
            print(f"- {task}")
        print("\n")

# Display the kanban board
display_kanban_board(tasks)
```

` ` `

Benefits of Agile in Supply Chains: Agile tools help supply chain professionals manage complex projects by breaking them down into smaller, more manageable parts. This modularity allows for adjustments to be made as new information comes to light, without derailing the entire project. Agile tools also foster better stakeholder engagement and accountability, as progress is transparent and team members can see how their contributions fit into the wider project goals.

Challenges to Implementation: Implementing Agile tools in supply chains can be challenging, particularly in traditional environments that are accustomed to rigid, linear project management approaches. There may be resistance to change, a lack of understanding of the Agile principles, or simply a dearth of experience with the tools themselves.

Scrum in Supply Chain Projects: Scrum, a subset of Agile, is another tool that can be applied to supply chain management. It organizes work in "sprints"—short, consistent periods during which specific work has to be completed and made ready for review. Scrum ceremonies, like daily stand-ups and sprint reviews, keep the project moving forward and ensure any issues are addressed promptly.

Collaborative Platforms: Today's market offers numerous Agile project management platforms that integrate with supply chain management systems. These platforms can track the progress of deliverables, manage backlogs, and facilitate the Scrum or kanban methodologies. They provide a centralized location for project documentation, which is vital for maintaining the institutional knowledge necessary for complex supply chain operations.

While Agile project management has its roots in software development, its principles are highly transferrable to supply chain projects. However, customization may be needed to accommodate the specific challenges and requirements of supply chains, such as regulatory compliance, global coordination, and physical logistics constraints.

Agile project management tools offer a powerful way to increase responsiveness and efficiency in supply chains. By incorporating these tools, supply chain managers can improve collaboration, adapt to changing conditions, and deliver projects that meet the evolving needs of their customers. As the landscape of global commerce continues to evolve, the role of Agile in ensuring supply chain resilience and competitiveness cannot be overstated.

Waste Identification and Elimination

In a world where resources are finite and consumer demand for sustainability is ever-increasing, the ability to identify and eliminate waste within supply chains is not just a cost-saving measure—it's an imperative for social responsibility and environmental stewardship.

Lean Principles in Supply Chains: The concept of waste elimination is deeply rooted in Lean management principles. Lean supply chain management targets waste in all its forms, whether it be excess inventory, unnecessary transport, or inefficient processes that consume more time and resources than they're worth.

1. Transport – Moving products unnecessarily.

2. Inventory – Holding more stock than necessary.

3. Motion – Unnecessary movements by people.

4. Waiting – Idle time created when waiting.

5. Overproduction – Producing more than what's required.

6. Over-processing – More work or higher quality than is demanded.

7. Defects – Effort involved in inspecting and fixing errors.

Identifying Waste: The first step in waste elimination is identification. In supply chains, this often involves mapping out the entire process, from raw material procurement to product delivery, and scrutinizing each step for inefficiencies.

```python
# A Python script to create a process map for supply chain visualization

    self.name = name
    self.inputs = inputs
    self.outputs = outputs
    self.time_taken = time_taken

    return f"{self.name}(Time: {self.time_taken} hrs, Inputs: {self.inputs}, Outputs: {self.outputs})"

# Define the supply chain process steps
procurement = ProcessStep('Procurement', ['Orders'], ['Raw Materials'], 24)

manufacturing = ProcessStep('Manufacturing', ['Raw Materials'], ['Products'], 48)
```

```
delivery = ProcessStep('Delivery', ['Products'], ['Delivered
Products'], 72)

# Create a list of process steps
process_chain = [procurement, manufacturing, delivery]

# Function to display the process map
    print(step)

# Display the process map
display_process_map(process_chain)
` ` `
```

Eliminating Waste: Once waste has been identified, the next step is to eliminate it. This may involve redesigning processes to be more efficient, investing in new technologies, or retraining staff to prevent defects and reduce motion and waiting times.

Continuous Improvement—Kaizen: Kaizen, or continuous improvement, is an integral component of Lean and is essential for waste elimination. By fostering a culture that encourages regular assessment and refinement, organizations can sustain gains made from eliminating waste and continue to find new areas for improvement.

To measure the success of waste elimination efforts, supply chain managers must establish clear metrics and key performance indicators (KPIs). These could include cycle time, cost of quality, or inventory turnover rates. By monitoring these KPIs, managers can quantify the impact of their waste elimination initiatives and justify further investment in Lean practices.

Resistance to change, especially in established supply chains, can be a significant hurdle. Additionally, identifying waste requires a deep understanding of the end-to-end process, which may be obscured by complex or siloed operations.

The elimination of waste is a journey toward efficiency and sustainability. By leveraging Lean principles and continuous improvement practices, supply chains can reduce costs, increase customer satisfaction, and contribute to a more sustainable future. The ongoing process of identifying and eliminating waste is not merely an operational challenge—it is a strategic endeavor that can define the competitive edge and environmental footprint of a company.

Resilience through Lean and Agile Practices

In the current marketplace, where disruptions are not the exception but the norm, supply chains must not only be efficient but also resilient. Resilience in this context speaks to the supply chain's ability to quickly recover from setbacks and adapt to change. Lean and Agile practices, while distinct, can be intertwined to create supply chains that are both streamlined and flexible.

Lean for Efficiency: Lean practices aim to create value by eliminating waste and optimizing processes. This results in a supply chain that is streamlined and cost-effective. For instance, just-in-time (JIT) inventory strategies can reduce waste associated with overstocking and minimize the financial burden of excess inventory.

Agile for Flexibility: On the other hand, Agile methodologies emphasize the ability to move quickly and easily in response to changing conditions. An Agile supply chain is characterized by its responsiveness to customer demands and its ability to pivot when faced with unforeseen events.

Combining Lean and Agile: The fusion of Lean and Agile methodologies can yield a supply chain that is both lean, in terms of waste reduction, and agile, in its capacity to adapt. This combination helps to buffer against volatility by allowing supply chains to respond dynamically to variations in demand and supply.

```python
# A Python script to manage inventory levels using Lean and
Agile practices

    self.safety_stock = safety_stock
    self.inventory_levels = {}

    self.inventory_levels[product_id] = quantity

    optimal_order = max(demand_forecast * lead_time -
self.inventory_levels.get(product_id, 0) + self.safety_stock, 0)
    return optimal_order

# Initialise inventory manager with a safety stock level
inventory_manager = InventoryManager(safety_stock=50)

# Update current inventory levels
inventory_manager.update_inventory('Widget', 100)
```

```
# Calculate stock order based on demand forecast and lead time
lead_time = 2  # Lead time in weeks
demand_forecast = 75  # Forecasted demand per week
order_quantity = inventory_manager.order_stock('Widget',
demand_forecast, lead_time)

print(f"Order quantity for Widget: {order_quantity}")
```
```

**Resilience through Adaptability**: Lean and Agile practices foster resilience not only through operational tactics but also by instilling a mindset of adaptability in the workforce. This cultural aspect ensures that employees are empowered to make decisions that align with the overall strategic goals of the supply chain.

**Risk Management**: A critical aspect of resilience is risk management. By identifying potential risks and developing contingency plans, supply chains can mitigate the impact of disruptions. Lean and Agile practices contribute to risk management by promoting end-to-end supply chain visibility and enabling rapid response to changes.

**Balancing Lean and Agile**: The challenge lies in balancing the two approaches. Lean focuses on reducing buffers, which can leave a supply chain vulnerable to disruptions. Agile practices, conversely, often involve maintaining certain buffers to enhance flexibility. Finding the right balance is crucial for building resilience without sacrificing efficiency.

In an unpredictable business landscape, resilience has become a cornerstone of supply chain strategy. By integrating Lean and
```

Agile practices, organizations can create supply chains that are not only efficient but also equipped to weather disruptions and bounce back stronger. It is this symbiotic relationship between the two methodologies that enables a supply chain to thrive amidst the complexities of the modern world.

CHAPTER 8: CUSTOMER-CENTRIC SUPPLY CHAIN ANALYTICS

*Understanding the Voice of
the Customer (VOC)*

The Voice of the Customer (VOC) is a term that encapsulates the detailed needs, wants, expectations, and preferences of a business's customers. In the realm of supply chain analytics, tapping into VOC is paramount for aligning operations with customer satisfaction and competitive advantage.

An effective VOC strategy involves a multifaceted approach to data collection. Surveys, focus groups, and direct interviews offer qualitative insights, while transactional data, customer service interactions, and digital footprints provide quantitative evidence of customer behavior. Each data stream contributes to a composite understanding of customer needs.

Once collected, the data must be meticulously analyzed to detect patterns and trends. Advanced analytics techniques, including sentiment analysis, text analytics, and machine learning algorithms, are employed to interpret the large volumes of unstructured data that VOC can encompass. These techniques facilitate the discovery of emerging customer demands, pain points, and preferences.

The insights gained from VOC are leveraged to drive strategic decision-making. For instance, a recurring complaint about late deliveries could indicate a need for supply chain optimization. Conversely, positive feedback on product quality may lead to reinforcing practices that maintain high standards. Supply chain analytics, therefore, becomes instrumental in converting VOC into operational improvements and innovation.

Python, with its comprehensive libraries like NumPy, pandas, and scikit-learn, serves as a powerful tool to process and analyze VOC data. Through Python's capabilities, one can create predictive models that forecast customer behavior, simulate the outcomes of different supply chain configurations, and provide prescriptive analytics for enhancing customer experience.

For example, using the pandas library, a data analyst can aggregate customer feedback from various channels and merge it with operational data to identify correlations between supply chain activities and customer satisfaction levels. The integration of data analysis with supply chain operations ensures that customer-centric metrics inform continuous improvement.

Incorporating VOC into the supply chain not only optimizes operations but also builds a customer-centric culture. It encourages organizations to view their supply chain through the lens of customer impact, ensuring that every link in the chain contributes to delivering value. By prioritizing VOC, businesses can achieve agility in responding to market changes and foster enduring customer relationships.

In summary, understanding the Voice of the Customer is a critical component in sculpting a responsive and competitive supply chain. Through thorough analysis and the application of analytical tools such as Python, supply chain professionals can distill vast quantities of customer data into strategic insights. These insights pave the way for a supply chain that not only meets but anticipates customer needs, thereby delivering exceptional value and fostering loyalty.

Customer Journey Mapping and Analytics

The practice of customer journey mapping marks a pivotal stride in decoding the myriad interactions a customer has with a brand. This visual representation of the customer's experience from initial contact through the various touchpoints to the ultimate endpoint – be it a purchase, a service completion, or beyond – is a critical tool in the supply chain analyst's arsenal.

Embarking on customer journey mapping starts with the identification of key customer segments and the paths they traverse within the business ecosystem. The journey encompasses multiple stages – awareness, consideration, purchase, service, and loyalty – each offering distinct opportunities for data capture and analysis. The map serves as a blueprint that reveals the points of interaction that are crucial to customer satisfaction and areas where the supply chain can be optimized to better serve these moments.

Analytics plays a vital role in enriching customer journey maps by providing a deeper layer of insight into customer behavior. For example, by analyzing purchase history data and customer service interactions, analysts can identify common bottlenecks that cause frustration or drop-offs. With this knowledge, supply chain processes can be refined to remove obstacles and streamline the customer's progression through the journey.

Python's analytical prowess is again leveraged here, with libraries such as Matplotlib and Seaborn enabling the visualization of complex customer journey data. Analysts can use these tools to create dynamic journey maps that highlight key metrics such as conversion rates, average time in each stage, and customer feedback scores.

Beyond visualization, predictive analytics can forecast future customer behaviors based on historical data, allowing supply chain adjustments before issues manifest. For instance, machine learning models can predict peak times for customer service inquiries and adjust inventory and staffing levels in anticipation. This proactive approach ensures the supply chain is robust and responsive to customer needs at every juncture.

One illustrative example involves leveraging the scikit-learn library to build classification models that predict which customers are likely to experience service issues based on their journey patterns. By identifying these customers early, supply chain managers can initiate targeted interventions to prevent dissatisfaction and enhance the customer experience.

Customer journey mapping and analytics, thus, provide a strategic framework for understanding and improving the end-to-end customer experience. This comprehensive overview allows supply chain managers to make informed decisions that align operational efficiency with customer-centric objectives. The result is a more nimble, customer-responsive supply chain that can adapt to the evolving landscape of customer expectations and maintain a competitive edge in the market.

In essence, marrying customer journey mapping with robust analytics transforms raw data into a narrative of the customer experience. This narrative empowers supply chain professionals to craft a seamless flow of interactions that not only meets customer expectations but also anticipates future needs, securing customer satisfaction and loyalty as a cornerstone of business success.

Personalization and Mass Customization Techniques

In a market where customer preferences shift with the speed of thought, personalization and mass customization stand as the twin pillars supporting the pursuit of customer delight. This section delves into the strategies and technologies enabling businesses to tailor products and services to individual preferences at scale, transforming the supply chain into a responsive and customer-centric entity.

Personalization, in the context of supply chain analytics, refers to the use of data-driven insights to create a unique value proposition for each customer. This approach requires a deep understanding of customer data, including demographics, purchasing patterns, and preferences. By leveraging this data, companies can customize their marketing, sales, and even product development to align closely with the customer's desires.

Mass customization is the natural extension of personalization. It represents the ability to produce goods and services to meet individual customer requirements with near mass production efficiency. This is achieved through modular design, flexible manufacturing processes, and advanced logistics. The result is a highly diversified array of products that can be rapidly assembled or configured according to specific customer demands.

Python, with its vast array of data analysis and machine learning libraries, is at the forefront of enabling these techniques. For instance, the use of Python's pandas library to segment customer data and identify unique buying patterns allows for the creation of personalized product bundles. Similarly, Python's scikit-learn library can help develop recommendation systems that suggest products or modifications, based on customer data, enhancing the mass customization process.

One innovative application of these techniques involves using machine learning to optimize supply chain decisions in real-time. An algorithm could, for example, dynamically adjust the production schedule and inventory levels for different product configurations, based on changing customer orders and preferences. This ensures that the supply chain can respond swiftly to individualized demands without sacrificing operational efficiency.

Furthermore, advancements in 3D printing and robotics have made it possible to produce customized products on-demand. These technologies integrate seamlessly with supply chain systems, allowing for the rapid production of items that are tailored to the customer's specifications. The incorporation of Internet of Things (IoT) devices within the supply chain further enhances the capability for personalization by providing real-time data on customer usage and product performance.

A case in point is the fashion industry, which has begun to harness these techniques to offer custom-fit clothing. By analyzing customer measurements and style preferences through Python-powered algorithms, companies can produce clothing that not only fits perfectly but also aligns with the customer's fashion sensibilities. The result is a highly personalized product, delivered with the efficiency of a standardized supply chain.

The fusion of personalization and mass customization techniques represents a paradigm shift in supply chain management. It challenges traditional one-size-fits-all production models and places the customer at the heart of the supply chain. By embracing these practices, companies not only meet the individual needs of their customers but also foster a sense of uniqueness and value that engenders brand loyalty and competitive differentiation.

In summation, personalization and mass customization are more than mere trends; they are reflections of a consumer-driven market that demands attention to individuality. As supply chains evolve to meet these demands, they become more agile, innovative, and attuned to the nuances of customer satisfaction. This transition, underpinned by sophisticated analytics and flexible manufacturing techniques, marks a bold step toward a future where every customer can truly say, "This was made for me."

Omni-Channel Supply Chain Strategies

In the tapestry of modern retail, omni-channel strategies thread together diverse shopping channels to create a seamless customer experience. As consumers increasingly expect fluidity between online, mobile, and in-store interactions, supply chains must adapt to deliver a cohesive service that blurs the lines between the physical and digital worlds.

Omni-channel supply chain strategies revolve around the core principle of meeting customers where they are, providing a consistent brand experience regardless of the platform or touchpoint. Achieving this requires a profound transformation in supply chain logistics, where flexibility and real-time responsiveness are paramount.

The foundational element of an omni-channel strategy is inventory visibility. It is essential for businesses to have a unified view of stock across all channels to meet customer expectations for product availability. Python can play a pivotal role here; utilizing databases and data analytics frameworks like SQLAlchemy and Pandas, businesses can aggregate inventory data from various sources, providing accurate, real-time insight into stock levels.

This visibility enables key omni-channel tactics such as buy online, pick up in-store (BOPIS), and ship from store, which leverage the retail network as a distributed fulfillment center. Advanced analytics, often facilitated by Python's powerful data manipulation capabilities, can predict optimal inventory distribution across channels to meet demand patterns, thus reducing delivery times and costs.

Furthermore, an effective omni-channel strategy needs to integrate reverse logistics seamlessly. Returns are a critical component of customer satisfaction, and managing them efficiently across all channels can be a complex challenge. Employing machine learning algorithms, businesses can analyze return patterns and reasons, optimizing the return process, and reducing the associated costs and impact on the supply chain.

A crucial enabler of omni-channel strategies is the integration of ERP and WMS systems with online platforms, which ensures that order management is synchronized across all channels. Technologies such as Python's Django framework can be used to develop web applications that interface with these systems, providing a unified dashboard for managing orders, inventory, and customer data.

Another aspect to consider is the role of the last mile delivery in shaping customer perceptions. With the advent of real-time tracking and same-day delivery expectations, supply chains must employ sophisticated route optimization algorithms. Tools like Google OR-Tools, implemented through Python, offer advanced route planning capabilities, improving delivery efficiency and customer satisfaction.

The success of omni-channel strategies is also contingent on robust customer data analytics. By analyzing customer interactions and purchase history, businesses can gain insights into shopping behavior and preferences. Python libraries like TensorFlow or PyTorch can be used to develop predictive models that personalize customer interactions and promotions across channels, further driving engagement and sales.

In practice, an omni-channel approach was exemplified by a major retailer that integrated its online and physical store inventory, allowing customers to view real-time stock at their local stores online. By implementing a flexible supply chain that could replenish stock quickly based on online and in-store demand signals, the retailer was able to promise and fulfill same-day in-store pickup for a wide range of products.

The omni-channel paradigm requires supply chains to be agile, technology-driven, and customer-centric. In this connected environment, each part of the supply chain is a step in the customer's journey, and excellence in delivery at each phase is crucial. The strategies and technologies discussed not only streamline operations but also enhance the customer's experience, fostering loyalty and driving growth in a fiercely competitive retail landscape.

Last Mile Delivery Analytics

The crescendo of any product's journey, the last mile of delivery, stands as a critical frontier in the realm of supply chain analytics. It is within this final stretch that customer expectations peak and the efficiency of logistical execution is put to the test. Last mile delivery analytics harnesses data to orchestrate and refine this crucial phase, ensuring that the culmination of the supply chain process is marked by punctuality and precision.

The art of optimizing last mile delivery begins with a granular analysis of delivery routes and customer locations. Here, geospatial data, when interwoven with historical traffic patterns and delivery times, can be transformed into actionable intelligence. Python's rich ecosystem, including libraries such as Geopandas and Folium, allows for the manipulation and visualization of such data, enabling logistics planners to craft the most efficient routes.

Moreover, customer expectations have transcended mere delivery of goods. They now encompass a desire for transparency and communication throughout the delivery process. Analytics plays a pivotal role in meeting these expectations by predicting delivery windows more accurately and providing real-time updates to customers. Machine learning models, developed using scikit-learn or TensorFlow, can learn from vast datasets of delivery timings, weather conditions, and traffic disruptions to enhance the accuracy of delivery predictions.

In tandem with predictive analytics, real-time tracking systems are invaluable. These systems, fed by GPS data and IoT devices, can generate a continual stream of data that, when processed instantaneously, ensures that customers are kept in the loop and any delivery issues can be proactively addressed. Python's capabilities for handling streaming data, through frameworks such as Apache Kafka and PySpark, make it an ideal choice for building robust tracking systems.

The efficiency of last mile delivery is not solely determined by the speed and accuracy of the delivery itself, but also by the successful completion of the delivery—the first time. Failed delivery attempts add cost and complexity to logistics operations. Data analytics can pinpoint the common causes of failed deliveries, such as incorrect addresses or customer unavailability, and through predictive modeling, suggest corrective actions such as optimal delivery times or alternative secure locations for parcel drop-off.

Sustainability also emerges as a paramount concern in last mile delivery. Fuel consumption and carbon emissions are closely scrutinized, and analytics can guide the adoption of eco-friendly practices. Route optimization algorithms not only reduce delivery times but also minimize environmental impact. Electric and alternative fuel vehicles, whose deployment can be planned and assessed through analytics, further contribute to a greener last mile.

A case in point of last mile delivery analytics at work is that of a logistics company that implemented dynamic route optimization, leading to a reduction in delivery times by 20%. They utilized predictive analytics to offer customers one-hour delivery windows with 95% accuracy, thus significantly enhancing customer satisfaction. Additionally, by analyzing delivery data, they were able to increase their first-time delivery success rate, resulting in lower costs and a reduced carbon footprint.

To sum up, last mile delivery analytics is an essential component of a streamlined supply chain, melding advanced data analysis with practical execution. It is the key to unlocking not only operational efficiencies but also to elevating the customer experience to new heights. By applying the analytical techniques and technologies mentioned, businesses can ensure that the journey of their products concludes as planned, leaving a lasting impression of excellence in the minds of their customers.

Customer Service and Retention Analytics

In the competitive tapestry of modern commerce, where products are often commoditized, the distinction often lies in the quality of customer service. Excelling in this domain not only satisfies consumers but also fosters loyalty and retention. The application of analytics to customer service and retention is the linchpin in developing a nuanced understanding of customer interactions, preferences, and pain points.

Delving into the heart of customer service analytics entails an exploration of data collected from multiple touchpoints – be it call centers, emails, social media interactions, or direct feedback.

The aggregation and analysis of this data, which can be adeptly handled by Python's pandas library, provides a comprehensive view of the customer's experience and journey. From here, one can glean insights into the effectiveness of customer service protocols and identify areas ripe for improvement.

One of the most potent tools within customer service analytics is sentiment analysis. By implementing natural language processing (NLP) techniques, businesses can interpret the underlying sentiment in customer communications, distinguishing between positive, neutral, and negative feedback. Tools such as NLTK or spaCy in Python enable the breakdown and categorization of sentiments, revealing trends that could prompt proactive measures to enhance service quality.

To enhance customer retention, churn prediction models are indispensable. These predictive models, often constructed using machine learning algorithms, can sift through historical data to identify customers at high risk of churn. Factors such as frequency of service issues, response times, and customer satisfaction scores are considered to forecast the likelihood of a customer severing ties. Through libraries such as XGBoost or PyTorch, one can develop these models, which in turn inform targeted retention strategies.

A practical application of these analytical approaches is found in the design of personalized customer service. By understanding individual customer behavior and preferences, service can be tailored to meet specific needs, thus deepening the customer's connection to the brand. For instance, a customer with a history of technical issues might receive proactive outreach when a new software update is released, thus pre-empting potential difficulties.

Investing in analytics also pays dividends in the refinement of customer service training programs. By identifying common queries and challenges, training can be focused on equipping service representatives with the skills and knowledge most pertinent to customer needs. This targeted education, informed by data, ensures that the service team is not only competent but also confident in their ability to resolve issues effectively.

The efficacy of customer service and retention analytics is perhaps best exemplified by a case study involving a retail company that implemented a comprehensive analytics dashboard. This dashboard synthesized data from various customer service channels, providing real-time insights into performance metrics and customer sentiment. The result was a 30% improvement in response times and a 10% increase in customer retention rates within six months of implementation.

Customer service and retention analytics stand as a dynamic and transformative element of business strategy. The judicious application of data analysis fortifies the customer service framework, ensuring that each customer interaction is both impactful and insightful. It is through this meticulous orchestration of data-driven initiatives that companies can secure the loyalty of their customers, thereby sustaining their competitive edge in today's market.

Sentiment Analysis and Customer Feedback

Pivoting towards sentiment analysis, we delve deeper into the realm where data intersects with human emotion. Here, customer feedback serves as a rich repository of insights, mirroring the voice of the consumer in raw, often unstructured data. Sentiment analysis, powered by the latest in artificial intelligence, harnesses this data, translating it into actionable business intelligence.

Let us consider the Python ecosystem, a fertile ground where libraries like TextBlob and Gensim thrive, enabling us to execute complex sentiment analysis with relative ease. By harnessing these tools, we can programmatically assess feedback and discern the sentiment that pervades customer reviews, social media comments, and survey responses. This analysis unveils not just the overt messages but also the subtle undertones that influence customer perception.

Imagine a scenario where a retail brand receives mixed feedback across various online platforms. Through sentiment analysis, the brand can quantify and categorize these sentiments, identifying prevailing attitudes towards their products or services. By conducting a temporal analysis, the brand could also track changes in sentiment over time, correlating them with specific campaigns, product launches, or service changes.

The real power of sentiment analysis lies in its ability to preempt dissatisfaction. By flagging negative sentiments early, businesses can swiftly address issues before they escalate. For example, a spike in negative sentiment around a product might prompt an immediate quality review, or a pattern of dissatisfaction with customer service could lead to a revamp of support protocols.

Moreover, sentiment analysis can enrich customer profiles, contributing to a more tailored marketing approach. Python's powerful data manipulation capabilities, through libraries like pandas, allow for the categorization of customers based on sentiment. This segmentation enables personalized marketing initiatives that resonate more deeply with each group's emotional triggers and preferences.

Transitioning from the micro to the macro, sentiment analysis also informs broader market research. When aggregated, customer sentiment can reveal market trends, brand health, and competitive positioning. Insights derived from such analysis can influence strategic decisions, such as product development directions or market entry strategies.

To illustrate this, consider a technology firm that, through sentiment analysis, discovers a growing demand for privacy features among its user base. Responding to this sentiment, the firm could prioritize the development of privacy-centric products, thus aligning their offerings with consumer sentiment and gaining a competitive advantage.

In essence, sentiment analysis is the compass that guides businesses through the vast sea of customer feedback. It converts the cacophony of customer voices into a symphony of insights, each note informing a more nuanced understanding of the market. By leveraging the power of Python and its libraries, businesses can navigate this domain with precision, ensuring that they remain attuned to the evolving sentiments of their customer base.

Demand-Driven Supply Chain Models

In the ever-evolving landscape of supply chain management, demand-driven models have emerged as a beacon of responsiveness, aligning the flow of goods to the ebb and flow of market demand. These models mark a paradigm shift from traditional supply-focused approaches, advocating for a pull-based strategy where consumer demand triggers supply chain activities.

The ethos of a demand-driven supply chain is predicated on visibility, agility, and synchronization. Central to this model is the concept of Demand Signal Repositories (DSRs), which aggregate real-time data from various consumer-facing channels. These repositories act as the nerve center for demand-driven operations, informing all subsequent supply chain actions.

Incorporating Python into this model, we can utilize its data analytics prowess to parse through vast datasets within DSRs. Python's libraries, such as NumPy for numerical computations and Matplotlib for data visualization, become instrumental in interpreting demand signals. By applying statistical analysis or machine learning algorithms, we can forecast demand more accurately and dynamically adjust supply chain activities.

Consider a consumer electronics company that employs a demand-driven model. By leveraging real-time sales data, social media analytics, and retailer inventory levels, the company can anticipate demand surges for specific products, such as a new smartphone release. Python scripts, running complex algorithms, can analyze these signals to optimize inventory distribution, ensuring that stock is replenished where demand is projected to spike.

Beyond inventory management, demand-driven models enhance the entire supply chain's responsiveness. For instance, a sudden uptick in demand for a fashion retailer can trigger an accelerated production schedule. Python can be used to develop simulation models that help decision-makers evaluate various scenarios, such as ramping up production or rerouting shipments to meet the unexpected demand.

These models also advocate for a more collaborative approach across the supply chain. By sharing demand insights with suppliers and logistics partners, a company can foster a cohesive response to market fluctuations. Python's ability to integrate with APIs facilitates the seamless exchange of data across different entities, enabling a synchronized response to demand signals.

Moreover, demand-driven supply chains are inherently customer-centric. By focusing on actual consumption instead of forecasts, companies can reduce the risk of overstocking or stockouts, leading to higher customer satisfaction. Python's data analysis capabilities can be used to segment customers and tailor supply chain operations to the preferences and behaviors of different customer groups.

In the context of sustainability, demand-driven models also present an opportunity to minimize waste. By aligning production and distribution closely with consumption patterns, companies can reduce excess inventory and the associated resource wastage. Python's analytics can play a pivotal role in achieving these sustainability goals by identifying optimal production levels and distribution strategies that align with environmental objectives.

A demand-driven supply chain is not without its challenges, however. It requires a robust technological infrastructure capable of handling real-time data and complex analytics. Herein lies the strategic role of Python, with its extensive libraries and community support, acting as a linchpin for implementing and managing demand-driven supply chain models effectively.

In conclusion, demand-driven supply chain models represent a transformative approach to managing the intricate dance of supply and demand. Through the astute application of Python and its analytical capabilities, businesses can navigate this landscape with a newfound agility, ensuring they are always a step ahead in meeting the needs of the ever-discerning customer.

Customer Lifetime Value (CLV) in Supply Chain Decisions

In the intricate tapestry of supply chain management, understanding the Customer Lifetime Value (CLV) is pivotal for shaping strategic decisions that extend beyond immediate profitability. CLV is a metric that represents the total revenue a business can reasonably expect from a single customer account throughout the business relationship. By infusing CLV into supply chain decisions, companies can transform their operations from transactional interactions into long-term customer-centric strategies.

The incorporation of CLV into supply chain decisions necessitates a deep dive into data analytics, a domain where Python excels with its extensive ecosystem of libraries and tools. By employing Python for predictive modeling, companies can estimate CLV with greater accuracy and granularity. Libraries such as Pandas for data manipulation, SciKit-Learn for machine learning, and Lifetimes for survival analysis come together to build a nuanced model of customer behavior.

Imagine a retail brand that has invested in understanding the CLV of its customer base. Through predictive analytics, the brand identifies that customers who purchase a particular range of products are likely to have a higher CLV. With this insight, supply chain decisions can be tailored to prioritize the availability of these high-impact products, optimizing inventory levels and allocation to meet the demands of high-value customers.

Furthermore, the insights gleaned from CLV can inform not just inventory decisions but also the design of tailored marketing campaigns, loyalty programs, and personalized customer service initiatives. This is where Python's capabilities in processing large datasets and automating data workflows empower businesses to act on CLV insights efficiently.

For instance, a company might use the CLV model to segment customers into different tiers based on their projected value. This segmentation allows for differentiated supply chain strategies, such as offering premium shipping options to high-tier customers, which enhances their experience and fosters loyalty. Python can automate the segmentation process and integrate it with customer relationship management (CRM) systems to deliver a seamless operational response.

Moreover, understanding CLV aids in making risk-adjusted supply chain decisions. High CLV customers might justify the investment in more resilient supply chain practices, such as dual sourcing or holding safety stock to ensure service level agreements are met. Python's simulation libraries, like SimPy, enable companies to model various risk scenarios and their impact on customer satisfaction and CLV.

The alignment of supply chain practices with CLV also highlights the role of personalization. As businesses strive to deliver personalized experiences, the supply chain must adapt to support this objective. Python's data analytics tools can uncover patterns in customer preferences, enabling supply chains to become more flexible and responsive in providing customized product assortments and packaging.

Sustainability is another aspect where CLV can have a significant influence. Customers with a higher CLV may be more receptive to sustainable practices and products. Supply chains can leverage this by optimizing routes to reduce carbon footprint or investing in eco-friendly packaging, which can further enhance customer loyalty and lifetime value.

In the realm of supply chain finance, CLV can influence credit terms and payment structures offered to customers. By understanding the long-term value of customers, supply chains can balance the cost-to-serve with expected returns, making financially sound decisions that support both customer satisfaction and the bottom line.

In summary, Customer Lifetime Value is a critical metric that, when integrated into supply chain analytics, can revolutionize how businesses perceive and interact with their customers. Using Python to analyze and act upon CLV insights ensures that supply chain decisions are made with a view toward fostering lasting and profitable customer relationships. The strategic infusion of CLV into supply chain operations heralds a new era of customer-first thinking, rooted in data-driven precision and executed with personalized flair.

Enhancing Customer Experience through Analytics

In the modern commercial landscape, the customer experience (CX) has ascended to the forefront of strategic priorities. It is a multifaceted concept that encompasses every interaction a customer has with a business, from browsing a website to unboxing a product. Analytics, particularly when harnessed skillfully, is a potent tool for enriching this journey, transforming passive encounters into engaging narratives that resonate with the customer's expectations and values.

The enhancement of customer experience through analytics begins with the meticulous gathering and analysis of customer data. Each touchpoint is a source of invaluable insights, painting a detailed portrait of customer behaviors, preferences, and pain points. Python, with its array of data processing libraries like NumPy and Pandas, stands as the cornerstone of this endeavor, facilitating the transformation of raw data into actionable knowledge.

One practical application is the customization of web interfaces using analytics. By analyzing browsing patterns and purchase histories, a business can tailor its website to display products and offers that align with individual customer profiles. Python's machine learning libraries, such as TensorFlow and Keras, allow for the creation of recommendation systems that not only enhance the user experience but also increase the likelihood of conversion.

The power of analytics extends to the physical realm as well. In brick-and-mortar stores, sensor data can be analyzed to optimize store layouts, ensuring that high-demand products are easily accessible, and the flow of foot traffic is unimpeded. Here, Python's data visualization tools, like Matplotlib and Seaborn, can convert complex datasets into intuitive graphical representations, making it easier for decision-makers to devise effective strategies.

Analytics also plays a pivotal role in personalizing communication with customers. By sifting through interaction histories, sentiment analysis algorithms can gauge the tone and content of past communications, enabling businesses to craft messages that resonate on a more personal level. Python's natural language processing libraries, such as NLTK and spaCy, are instrumental in automating and refining this process, ensuring that each customer feels heard and valued.

In the context of post-purchase support, analytics can be utilized to preemptively address potential issues. Predictive models can identify patterns that may lead to customer dissatisfaction, prompting proactive measures such as sending care tips for products or reminders for maintenance. Python's predictive modeling capabilities ensure that these interventions are timely and relevant, fostering a sense of care that customers appreciate.

Moreover, the integration of analytics into customer feedback loops is essential. Surveys, product reviews, and social media comments are rich with insights that can drive continuous improvement. Text analytics can distill this feedback into themes and trends, directing attention to areas that need enhancement. Python's versatility in handling diverse data types ensures that no piece of feedback is left unexamined.

The culmination of these efforts is the creation of a seamless and responsive customer journey. Each analytic-driven adjustment to products, services, or interactions is a step towards a more harmonious relationship with customers. As businesses strive to deliver not just products, but experiences, the symbiosis between the supply chain and customer experience becomes evident. Analytics, powered by Python, becomes the bridge connecting supply chain operations with the customer's world, ensuring that every decision is made with the ultimate goal of delivering delight and driving loyalty.

In this pursuit, it is crucial to remember that enhancing customer experience is an ongoing process, a relentless quest for excellence that requires continuous learning and adaptation. The analytics-driven approach to CX is not a one-time initiative but a cultural shift within the organization, one that places the customer at the heart of every decision, every innovation, and every touchpoint. Through the strategic use of analytics, businesses can not only meet but exceed customer expectations, securing their place in the competitive landscape of tomorrow.

CHAPTER 9: ADVANCED TECHNOLOGIES IN SUPPLY CHAIN ANALYTICS

Artificial Intelligence and Machine Learning Applications

The tapestry of contemporary supply chain management is richly interwoven with the threads of Artificial Intelligence (AI) and Machine Learning (ML), technologies that are revolutionizing the way organizations interpret data, make decisions, and manage their operations. Advancements in AI and ML have ushered in an era of unprecedented efficiency and intelligence, enabling supply chains to become more predictive, adaptive, and responsive to the dynamic market environment.

AI and ML applications in supply chain analytics are vast and transformative. One of the most significant contributions of AI is in the realm of demand forecasting. Traditional statistical methods, while robust, often fall short in capturing the nonlinear complexities of market demand. ML algorithms, such as recurrent neural networks (RNNs) and long short-term memory networks (LSTMs), excel in identifying patterns within large datasets that are too intricate for human analysts to discern. By leveraging Python's deep learning frameworks like TensorFlow, supply chain analysts can develop forecasting models that adapt and improve over time, reducing forecasting errors and enhancing inventory management.

Inventory management, too, is fertile ground for AI's capabilities. ML models can predict optimal stock levels by analyzing a multitude of factors, including seasonal trends, promotional activities, and even social media sentiment. By employing unsupervised learning techniques, such as clustering algorithms implemented in Python's scikit-learn library, businesses can categorize products based on variability in demand, leading to smarter inventory decisions that minimize holding costs and prevent stockouts.

In the sphere of logistics and transportation, AI-driven route optimization solutions are reshaping delivery networks. These solutions consider constraints such as traffic patterns, delivery windows, and vehicle load capacities, delivering plans that minimize travel time and fuel consumption. Python's optimization libraries, like SciPy and PuLP, are indispensable tools for building models that not only streamline delivery routes but also contribute to sustainability by reducing carbon emissions.

AI also amplifies capabilities in risk management. By utilizing a blend of predictive analytics and prescriptive analytics, AI systems can identify potential disruptions in the supply chain, from supplier insolvencies to natural disasters. Beyond risk identification, ML models can recommend mitigation strategies, drawing from historical data to suggest actions that have successfully navigated similar challenges in the past. Python's robust data analysis capabilities ensure that these systems are both comprehensive and precise, fostering resilience in supply chain operations.

Furthermore, AI plays a pivotal role in enhancing supplier relationships. Through the application of natural language processing (NLP), businesses can extract insights from supplier communications, contracts, and performance data, gaining a 360-degree view of supplier health and capabilities. Python's NLP libraries, like Gensim and TextBlob, enable the extraction of key phrases and sentiments, providing a deeper understanding of supplier dynamics and informing better partnership decisions.

In the context of quality control, computer vision, a subset of AI, is transforming inspection processes. By training ML models on images of products, these systems can detect defects and quality deviations with greater accuracy and consistency than human inspectors. Python's OpenCV library offers the tools necessary to develop these computer vision systems, which ultimately serve to elevate product quality and customer satisfaction.

The integration of AI and ML into supply chain analytics represents a paradigm shift towards more intelligent, data-driven decision-making. These technologies empower businesses to navigate complexity with agility and precision, turning vast streams of data into a competitive advantage. As the supply chain landscape continues to evolve, the strategic application of AI and ML will be critical in driving innovation, operational excellence, and value creation.

In synthesizing the potential of AI and ML with the pragmatic needs of supply chain management, it is evident that these technologies are not mere novelties but essential components of a modern supply chain's toolkit. They offer a means to transcend traditional limitations, enabling supply chains to anticipate the future and shape it proactively. The future of supply chain excellence is inseparable from the intelligent algorithms that will define it, and as professionals in the field, our quest is not just to understand these technologies but to master them, wielding them with skill and foresight to build the resilient, customer-centric supply chains of tomorrow.

Blockchain for Traceability and Transparency

In the ever-evolving landscape of supply chain management, the quest for traceability and transparency is paramount. Blockchain technology has emerged as a beacon of hope, offering an immutable ledger that provides an unassailable record of transactions, thereby enhancing visibility and trust across the supply chain network.

The very essence of blockchain is its distributed ledger technology (DLT), which allows for a secure and decentralized record-keeping system. Each 'block' of data is linked to the previous one, forming a 'chain' that is resistant to tampering and fraud. This architecture is particularly beneficial for supply chains, as it enables a transparent and verifiable history of products from origin to end-user, ensuring authenticity and compliance.

One of the most compelling applications of blockchain in supply chains is in the area of food safety. By tagging food products with unique digital identifiers and recording each step of their journey on the blockchain, it becomes possible to trace the provenance of food items in real-time. This can significantly reduce the time required to track and contain contamination issues, thus safeguarding public health and reinforcing consumer confidence. For instance, a Python-based smart contract on an Ethereum blockchain platform could automatically execute payments to suppliers once a delivery is verified, streamlining the process and reducing the potential for disputes.

Blockchain's applicability extends to the realm of ethical sourcing as well. Consumers and regulators are increasingly demanding transparency in sourcing practices, particularly concerning conflict minerals and fair labor conditions. Blockchain facilitates the creation of a transparent supply chain where the ethical credentials of a product, such as being conflict-free or sustainably sourced, can be verified by all stakeholders, including consumers. Python libraries like Web3.py can be utilized to interact with blockchain networks, enabling the integration of blockchain data with supply chain applications.

In the pharmaceutical industry, blockchain is poised to play a significant role in combatting counterfeit drugs. By recording the serial numbers of drug packages on a blockchain, stakeholders can authenticate the legitimacy of pharmaceutical products at every stage, from manufacturing to delivery to pharmacies. Python's Pandas library can be used to manage and analyze the data associated with these serial numbers, ensuring that only genuine products reach patients.

Moreover, blockchain enhances supply chain finance by simplifying transactions and reducing the need for intermediaries. Smart contracts, self-executing contracts with the terms directly written into code, can automate the execution of agreements upon the fulfillment of predefined conditions. This removes inefficiencies and the risk of manual errors in financial transactions. Python's Solidity libraries allow developers to deploy smart contracts on blockchain platforms, revolutionizing the way payments and financial agreements are handled in the supply chain.

The integration of blockchain into supply chain operations also addresses the challenge of compliance with regulations. By providing an immutable record of transactions, blockchain serves as a reliable source for audit trails. This facilitates compliance with regulations such as the Drug Supply Chain Security Act (DSCSA) and the Modern Slavery Act, which require detailed tracking and reporting of products and materials. By using Python to create blockchain-based compliance tools, companies can ensure that they meet regulatory standards more efficiently.

In the broader context of supply chain analytics, the incorporation of blockchain technology promises to enhance decision-making capabilities. With access to real-time, verifiable data, supply chain managers can make more informed decisions about sourcing, logistics, and risk management. Python's data visualization libraries, like Matplotlib and Seaborn, can be harnessed to present blockchain data in an accessible format, aiding in the analysis and communication of insights.

Blockchain technology is not without its challenges, including integration with legacy systems, scalability issues, and the need for widespread adoption to realize its full potential. Yet, its promise for creating more secure, transparent, and efficient supply chains is undeniable. As businesses seek to fortify their operations against fraud and disruptions, blockchain stands as a transformative force, a digital ledger not just of transactions, but of trust and integrity in the global marketplace.

As supply chain professionals, embracing blockchain technology is essential in our pursuit of excellence. Its potential to revolutionize the industry compels us to explore its applications and to develop the expertise necessary to implement it effectively. The path forward is one of collaboration and innovation, where blockchain becomes an integral part of our strategy to build supply chains that are not just efficient, but also ethical, sustainable, and resilient.

Advanced Predictive and Prescriptive Analytics

Advancements in predictive and prescriptive analytics have catalyzed a paradigm shift in how supply chain decisions are made. Where once decisions were guided by intuition and experience, they are now increasingly data-driven, with sophisticated models offering insights that can foresee future trends and prescribe actionable strategies.

Predictive analytics harness historical data to forecast future events with a considerable degree of accuracy. It uses statistical algorithms and machine learning techniques to identify the likelihood of future outcomes based on historical data. An example of this in Python could involve using the scikit-learn library to build a predictive model that forecasts demand based on past sales data, promotional schedules, and external factors like weather or economic indicators.

Prescriptive analytics goes a step further by not only predicting outcomes but also suggesting actions to benefit from the predictions. This branch of analytics uses a combination of business rules, algorithms, machine learning, and computational modelling techniques to recommend the best course of action for any pre-specified outcome. Using Python, one could leverage the PuLP library to solve complex optimization problems, such as determining the optimal inventory levels to minimize costs while avoiding stockouts.

1. **Optimizing Inventory Levels**: By predicting future demand with greater precision, businesses can maintain optimal inventory levels, achieving a balance between capital investment and service level. This is where predictive analytics can be invaluable, helping to reduce both overstock and stockouts, thus saving costs and improving customer satisfaction.

2. **Smarter Forecasting**: Predictive models can detect patterns and trends that humans may overlook. For example, machine learning models can analyze vast amounts of data to predict consumer buying behavior, helping companies adjust their supply chain strategies accordingly. This could involve using Python's TensorFlow or Keras libraries to build neural networks that can predict future purchasing patterns based on complex data sets.

3. **Enhanced Risk Management**: Prescriptive analytics can play a pivotal role in identifying potential risks in the supply chain and suggesting mitigation strategies. By simulating different scenarios, companies can prepare for and manage risks such as supplier failures, logistical delays, or sudden changes in demand.

4. **Dynamic Pricing Strategies**: Advanced analytics can enable dynamic pricing models that respond in real-time to changes in demand, competition, and market conditions. For instance, Python's NumPy and Pandas libraries can be used to analyze market data and adjust pricing to maximize profits or market share.

5. **Sustainable Operations**: Predictive analytics can also contribute to sustainability by optimizing routes to reduce fuel consumption or suggesting adjustments to production schedules to minimize energy usage. Python's geospatial libraries like GeoPandas can assist in route optimization to minimize carbon footprints.

6. **Customer-Centric Supply Chains**: By understanding and anticipating customer needs, predictive analytics can shape a supply chain that is more responsive and customer-focused. This might involve analyzing social media data using natural language processing (NLP) to gain insights into customer sentiment, using libraries like NLTK or spaCy in Python.

The potential of advanced analytics is not without its challenges. The complexity of predictive models can sometimes result in a 'black box' scenario, where the reasoning behind predictions and prescriptions is not transparent. Moreover, the success of these analytics hinges on the quality of data, which must be accurate, complete, and timely. Implementing such systems also requires a workforce skilled in data science and analytics, capable of interpreting the results and making informed decisions.

As we stand on the cusp of a new era in supply chain management, it is clear that embracing advanced predictive and prescriptive analytics is not merely an option but an imperative. The competitive edge gained through these analytical capabilities can lead to more agile, efficient, and customer-oriented supply chains. The journey towards harnessing the full potential of these technologies is an exciting and ongoing process, one that promises to redefine the horizons of supply chain excellence.

Augmented Reality (AR) and Virtual Reality (VR) in Warehousing

The application of Augmented Reality (AR) and Virtual Reality (VR) technologies is revolutionizing warehousing operations, offering immersive and interactive experiences that enhance efficiency and accuracy. These innovative technologies are not mere futuristic concepts but are currently being deployed to solve real-world challenges in the logistics and supply chain sector.

Augmented Reality (AR) overlays digital information onto the physical environment, typically through the use of headsets or smart glasses, which allows warehouse workers to interact with data in a hands-free, intuitive manner. For example, AR can project picking information directly into a worker's line of sight, guiding them to the correct location and verifying the right item is picked through barcode or RFID scanning. This streamlines the picking process, reduces errors, and improves worker productivity.

Consider a Python-based AR application where the warehouse worker's headset display is powered by a combination of the OpenCV library for image processing and the Pygame library for overlaying interactive graphics. This setup could guide workers through complex inventory layouts, ensuring that the path taken minimizes travel time and increases the speed of order fulfillment.

Virtual Reality (VR), on the other hand, creates a completely digital environment that users can interact with in a seemingly real way. VR is particularly useful for training purposes in warehousing. It can simulate a variety of scenarios, from everyday operations to emergency situations, allowing workers to gain experience in a safe, controlled virtual setting. Trainees can learn and practice the skills needed for efficient warehousing without the risk of accidents or damage to actual inventory.

For instance, a VR training program could be developed using Python's VR libraries such as PyVirtualDisplay and Vizard. In such a program, warehouse workers could practice navigating a virtual warehouse, learning the optimal routes and procedures for different tasks, which would lead to better performance in the actual work environment.

1. **Enhanced Training**: VR provides an immersive learning environment for new employees, significantly reducing the learning curve and the need for on-the-job training that could disrupt daily operations.

2. **Increased Productivity**: AR assists in picking and packing processes by providing real-time information, which reduces the time taken to locate items and ensures accuracy in order fulfillment.

3. **Improved Safety**: Both AR and VR can contribute to a safer workplace. AR can provide alerts and safety tips in real-time, while VR can prepare workers for emergency responses without exposing them to real dangers.

4. **Optimized Space Utilization**: VR can be used to design and test warehouse layouts virtually before implementing any physical changes. This ensures optimal space usage and workflow before any investment is made in restructuring.

5. **Remote Collaboration**: With AR, experts can remotely assist on-site workers through shared visuals, leading to more efficient problem-solving and maintenance.

6. **Error Reduction**: By integrating AR with existing Warehouse Management Systems (WMS), workers receive visual confirmations for tasks, which helps in minimizing picking and placement errors.

The integration of AR and VR into warehousing presents its set of challenges. It requires a significant investment in technology infrastructure and training to ensure that the workforce is comfortable and proficient in using these new tools. Furthermore, these technologies must be seamlessly integrated into existing systems to avoid disruptions in workflows and to truly enhance operations rather than complicate them.

Nevertheless, as warehousing operations continue to scale and the demand for faster and more accurate order fulfillment grows, the adoption of AR and VR stands as a testament to the innovative spirit driving the supply chain industry forward. These technologies not only improve the bottom line by optimizing operational efficiencies but also signify a commitment to continually improving the worker experience, safety, and skill development. The future of warehousing, augmented by AR and VR, is poised to be more interactive, efficient, and adaptable to the evolving demands of the global market.

Autonomous Vehicles and Drones in Distribution

The advent of autonomous vehicles and drones is transforming the distribution landscape, propelling the supply chain into a new era of efficiency and responsiveness. The integration of these advanced technologies into distribution networks is not just an enhancement to current systems but a complete reimagining of delivery mechanisms.

Autonomous vehicles, including self-driving trucks and delivery vans, leverage a combination of sensors, cameras, and artificial intelligence to navigate roads with little to no human intervention. The benefits of autonomous vehicles for distribution are manifold. They promise to reduce labor costs, minimize human error, increase road safety, and optimize delivery routes through advanced algorithms. For instance, companies can utilize Python's machine learning libraries, such as TensorFlow or Keras, to analyze vast datasets of delivery routes and traffic patterns, enabling these autonomous vehicles to determine the most efficient paths and schedules.

Drones, or unmanned aerial vehicles (UAVs), offer an even more radical departure from traditional delivery methods. Capable of vertical takeoff and landing, drones can access remote or hard-to-reach areas without the constraints of road infrastructure. They are particularly adept at last-mile deliveries, which are often the most time-consuming and expensive part of the distribution process. Python's drone programming libraries, like DroneKit or MAVProxy, enable the development of sophisticated flight control systems that can autonomously pilot drones to precise GPS coordinates while avoiding obstacles.

1. **Reduced Delivery Times**: Drones can quickly deliver goods to consumers' doorsteps, especially in urban areas, bypassing road congestion and reducing the overall time from order to delivery.

2. **Lower Operating Costs**: Autonomous vehicles can operate

continuously without the need for breaks, reducing the number of vehicles and drivers needed for a distribution fleet.

3. **Decreased Environmental Impact**: Electrically powered autonomous vehicles and drones contribute to lower carbon emissions, aligning with sustainability goals.

4. **Enhanced Customer Experience**: The novelty and precision of drone deliveries can improve customer satisfaction by offering faster, reliable service.

5. **Improved Inventory Management**: With the real-time tracking capabilities of autonomous vehicles and drones, companies gain better visibility into their inventory on the move, allowing for more accurate stock management.

6. **Accessibility to Remote Areas**: Drones are especially useful for delivering medical supplies and other critical items to areas that are difficult to access by traditional vehicles.

The deployment of autonomous vehicles and drones also presents a set of challenges that must be navigated. Regulatory hurdles, public safety concerns, and privacy issues are at the forefront of the conversation surrounding these technologies. Additionally, the current infrastructure may need substantial upgrades to accommodate the widespread use of autonomous vehicles and drones, including the development of dedicated charging stations and drone ports.

Moreover, cybersecurity becomes a critical consideration as these technologies rely heavily on data exchange and connectivity. Protecting the systems from hacking and ensuring data integrity is paramount to maintaining trust in these automated distribution methods.

Despite these challenges, the potential of autonomous vehicles and drones to revolutionize distribution is clear. As companies continue to invest in and develop these technologies, the future of distribution is set to become more agile, cost-effective, and customer-centric. The implementation of these cutting-edge solutions not only signifies a leap in operational capabilities but also a transformative step towards a more interconnected and automated global supply chain ecosystem.

Robotics and Automation in Supply Chains

Robotics and automation represent a significant technological leap in the realm of supply chain management. These innovations are reshaping the industry, offering unprecedented levels of precision, efficiency, and scalability. The use of robotics extends from the warehouse floor to the sorting centers and all the way to the point of delivery, automating processes that were once labor-intensive and prone to human error.

Warehouse robotics have seen a surge in implementation, with machines capable of performing a multitude of tasks such as picking and packing, sorting, and transporting goods. Robots equipped with advanced vision systems and gripping mechanisms can identify and handle products of varying shapes and sizes, a task that has traditionally been challenging for machines. Python's robotics libraries, such as PyRobot or ROSPy, allow developers to program these robots, providing a layer of intelligence that enables them to interact with their environment and make autonomous decisions.

Automation also comes in the form of sophisticated conveyor belts, automated guided vehicles (AGVs), and autonomous mobile robots (AMRs) that can navigate through warehouses without the need for extensive infrastructure changes. These systems are often integrated with a warehouse management system (WMS) and are instrumental in optimizing the flow of goods, reducing the time it takes for products to move from receiving to shipping.

1. **Increased Productivity**: Robots can work around the clock, handling repetitive tasks more quickly than human workers and boosting overall throughput.

2. **Enhanced Accuracy**: Automation reduces the likelihood of errors in order picking and inventory management, translating to higher customer satisfaction.

3. **Labor Cost Savings**: Although the initial investment in robotics may be significant, the long-term savings on labor can be substantial, especially in regions with high wages.

4. **Improved Worker Safety**: By taking on dangerous or physically demanding tasks, robots can help reduce workplace injuries and create a safer environment for employees.

5. **Scalability**: Automated systems can be scaled up or down to meet demand fluctuations, making them incredibly versatile for businesses of all sizes.

6. **Data Collection and Analysis**: Robotics systems are capable of gathering detailed data on warehouse operations, which can be analyzed to further refine processes and improve efficiency.

The integration of robotics and automation is not without its challenges. There is a need for skilled personnel to manage and maintain these systems, and the transition can be disruptive to existing workflows. Additionally, the human workforce may require retraining to take on new roles that focus on the oversight and maintenance of these automated systems.

Another consideration is the capital expenditure required to implement such technologies. While larger corporations may have the resources to invest in high-end robotic systems, small to medium-sized enterprises (SMEs) may find it more challenging to justify the cost. However, as a testament to the growing importance of robotics and automation, many companies are now offering Robotics-as-a-Service (RaaS) models, allowing businesses to deploy these solutions without the upfront costs.

The future trajectory of supply chain management is clear: robotics and automation will continue to advance and become even more integral to operations. As these technologies become more sophisticated and cost-effective, their adoption within supply chains will likely accelerate. This shift not only promises to enhance operational capacities but also to spur innovation in supply chain strategies, driving the industry towards a more responsive and resilient future.

Wearable Technologies for Workforce Analytics

The integration of wearable technologies into supply chain operations marks a transformative shift in how workforce analytics are gathered and utilized. These devices, which include smartwatches, fitness trackers, and body-mounted sensors, provide a conduit for capturing real-time data on worker activities, health, and safety. The granular insights derived from wearable tech offer a profound understanding of workforce dynamics and enable managers to streamline operations, bolster safety, and enhance productivity.

In the context of supply chain management, wearable devices serve multiple functions. They can track an employee's location within a warehouse, monitor vital signs to prevent heatstroke or fatigue, and even provide haptic feedback for navigation or task completion. Smart glasses and head-mounted displays offer hands-free access to information, allowing workers to receive real-time updates and instructions while they perform their tasks.

Python's role in this innovation is pivotal. With libraries such as TensorFlow for machine learning and Flask for creating web applications, developers can build systems that process the data collected from wearables to make predictive assessments about workforce efficiency and well-being. For instance, by analyzing the movement patterns of warehouse staff, a Python-powered algorithm can identify bottlenecks in workflows and suggest layout changes to optimize the path of travel.

1. **Enhanced Operational Efficiency**: By monitoring the pace and patterns of workers, wearables can help identify inefficiencies in processes and provide data-driven insights for improvements.

2. **Proactive Health Monitoring**: Continuous tracking of vital signs can alert managers to potential health issues before they escalate, ensuring the well-being of employees and reducing absenteeism.

3. **Safety Compliance**: Wearables can ensure that workers are adhering to safety protocols, such as lifting correctly or staying clear of hazardous zones.

4. Training and Onboarding: New employees can be guided through tasks via augmented reality (AR) wearables, reducing the learning curve and improving training outcomes.

5. Job Satisfaction and Engagement: Providing feedback and personal performance metrics can motivate workers and create a more engaging and rewarding work environment.

6. Personalized Ergonomics: Data on an individual's movements and exertions can lead to personalized recommendations for ergonomic adjustments, reducing the risk of strain and injury.

One of the challenges with wearable technology is ensuring user acceptance and managing privacy concerns. Employees may be apprehensive about being monitored continuously, and there must be clear policies in place regarding the collection, use, and security of personal data. Transparency in how the data will be used to improve both individual and organizational performance is key to gaining trust.

Moreover, the integration of wearable technology into existing IT infrastructures requires careful planning. There must be a robust data management strategy in place to handle the influx of information from these devices, necessitating investments in data storage, processing power, and cybersecurity.

The forward momentum of wearable technologies in the supply chain sector indicates a future where these devices become commonplace. Their ability to provide a detailed lens into workforce operations will be invaluable for companies seeking to remain competitive in an increasingly data-driven landscape. As the capabilities of these technologies advance, their role in workforce analytics will become more pronounced, offering deeper insights and fostering a more proactive approach to managing the human elements of the supply chain.

Digital Platforms and Ecosystems

The digitalization of supply chains has ushered in a new era characterized by interconnectedness and interdependence. Digital platforms and ecosystems stand at the forefront of this revolution, offering integrated solutions that connect various aspects of supply chain operations. The essence of these platforms is to facilitate collaboration, optimize processes, and deliver insights that drive strategic decision-making across the entire supply chain network.

A digital platform in the supply chain context is a technology-enabled tool that allows multiple participants, including suppliers, manufacturers, distributors, and retailers, to interact and conduct business in a virtual environment. These platforms can encompass procurement systems, cloud-based inventory management, transportation management systems, and customer engagement tools. They enable the seamless flow of information and goods by leveraging technologies like cloud computing, the Internet of Things (IoT), and advanced analytics.

One of the most significant advantages of digital platforms is the creation of a shared digital ecosystem that connects different stakeholders. This ecosystem facilitates real-time data sharing and collaboration, leading to more synchronized and responsive supply chains. By having access to shared data, companies can make more informed decisions, reduce redundancies, and identify synergies that can lead to cost savings and enhanced service levels.

Python's versatility as a programming language makes it an ideal candidate for developing such digital platforms. Its frameworks, such as Django for web development and Pandas for data manipulation, enable rapid development of robust and scalable digital solutions. For example, a Python-based platform can aggregate data from various sources, process it using machine learning algorithms, and provide predictive insights into consumer demand patterns, inventory levels, and potential supply disruptions.

1. **Data Integration**: Unifying data from disparate systems and sources to provide a holistic view of the supply chain.

2. **Collaboration Tools**: Enabling stakeholders to communicate and work together more effectively, breaking down silos and fostering a more integrated approach to supply chain management.

3. **Marketplaces**: Providing a digital space for buyers and sellers to connect, negotiate, and transact, thus expanding market reach and sourcing options.

4. **Visibility and Tracking**: Offering end-to-end visibility of the supply chain, from raw materials to the end customer, allowing for better monitoring and management of the flow of goods.

5. **Analytics and Intelligence**: Utilizing data to generate actionable insights, predict future trends, and support decision-making processes.

6. **Automation and Workflow Optimization**: Streamlining

operations by automating routine tasks and optimizing workflows for greater efficiency.

One illustrative example of a digital platform is an online freight marketplace that connects shippers with carriers. By using this platform, shippers can post their shipping needs, and carriers can bid on the jobs. Python-based algorithms can match shippers with the most suitable carriers based on factors such as cost, timing, and carrier performance ratings. This optimizes the shipping process, reduces empty miles for carriers, and helps shippers find competitive rates.

Implementing digital platforms and ecosystems is not without its challenges. Companies must navigate issues related to data governance, cybersecurity, and change management. There is also the need for standardization across the platform to ensure compatibility and interoperability between different systems and tools.

As supply chains continue to evolve, digital platforms and ecosystems will play an increasingly central role. They provide the infrastructure necessary for companies to adapt to the rapid pace of change in the global business environment. By leveraging these digital solutions, organizations can enhance connectivity, improve agility, and drive innovation, positioning themselves for success in the digital age.

Edge Computing in Logistics and Distribution

In the intricate dance of logistics and distribution, edge computing emerges as the pivotal technology that brings computational power closer to the source of data generation – the edge of the network. This shift towards decentralized computing architecture is not just a trend; it is revolutionizing how supply chains operate, offering enhanced speed, reliability, and operational efficiency.

At the heart of edge computing's value proposition is the ability to process and analyze data near its point of origin, thus reducing latency and bandwidth usage. In logistics and distribution, this means real-time data processing at warehouses, during transportation, and at retail sites. It empowers supply chain managers to make swift, informed decisions, a capability that is particularly crucial in time-sensitive environments.

The implementation of edge computing in logistics can be visualized through the deployment of IoT devices. These devices, equipped with sensors, are embedded across various assets like containers, pallets, or vehicles. They collect data on location, temperature, humidity, and other critical parameters. By processing this data locally, edge computing devices can trigger immediate actions, such as adjusting the temperature in a refrigerated truck if the cargo is at risk of spoilage, without the need to communicate with a central data center.

Python emerges again as a valuable tool in this ecosystem due to its vast libraries and frameworks that facilitate working with IoT data. Libraries such as NumPy for numerical data processing and PyTorch or TensorFlow for machine learning enable the development of sophisticated edge computing applications that can learn from data and improve decision-making over time.

1. **Enhanced Responsiveness**: Immediate data processing allows for quicker response times to changing conditions, critical in managing perishable goods or time-sensitive deliveries.

2. **Bandwidth Efficiency**: By processing data locally, less data needs to be transmitted over the network, conserving bandwidth and reducing costs.

3. **Improved Security**: Local data processing minimizes the risk of data interception during transmission, enhancing data security and privacy.

4. **Operational Continuity**: Edge computing can operate independently of the central network, ensuring continuity of operations even when connectivity is compromised.

5. **Scalability**: As logistics operations grow, edge computing nodes can be seamlessly added without significant changes to the central infrastructure.

Consider the application of edge computing in a distribution center. A fleet of autonomous guided vehicles (AGVs) outfitted with sensors navigates the warehouse, transporting goods from storage to loading docks. These AGVs use edge computing to process sensor data in real time, navigating the most efficient routes and avoiding obstacles without the need to communicate with a central server. This reduces delays and increases the throughput of the distribution center.

However, the adoption of edge computing also brings its own set of challenges. Ensuring the interoperability between various devices and systems, managing the large volumes of data generated, and maintaining these distributed computing nodes are areas that require careful consideration and strategic planning.

Furthermore, edge computing facilitates the move towards

a more proactive logistics strategy. Predictive maintenance of transportation vehicles is a prime example. By analyzing data directly from the vehicle's sensors, potential issues can be identified and addressed before they escalate into costly downtime. This predictive approach can lead to significant savings and increased vehicle availability.

As businesses strive to meet the ever-increasing demands for speed and customization in delivery services, edge computing stands as a technological ally. It paves the way to a future where logistics and distribution operations are not only reactive but predictive, capable of adapting to the dynamic needs of the market in the blink of an eye. The application of edge computing in logistics and distribution is a testament to the relentless pursuit of excellence in the supply chain, ensuring that products are delivered with unparalleled efficiency and precision.

Quantum Computing and Its Potential Impact

As we stand on the precipice of a new era in computational power, quantum computing emerges as the vanguard, poised to redefine the possibilities within logistics and distribution. This burgeoning technology operates on the principles of quantum mechanics, where qubits, unlike traditional bits, can exist in multiple states simultaneously, offering exponential increases in processing capabilities.

The potential of quantum computing in the realm of supply chain management is vast and varied. Its ability to solve complex optimization problems, which are currently intractable for classical computers, can lead to revolutionary improvements in route planning and inventory management. Quantum algorithms have the capability to analyze and optimize entire supply networks in moments, a task that would take contemporary systems considerably longer.

For logistics, the implications are profound. Quantum computing could enable the optimization of delivery routes considering thousands of vehicles and destinations, while also accounting for real-time traffic data, weather conditions, and vehicle performance metrics. This level of optimization could yield near-perfect efficiency, drastically reducing fuel consumption and delivery times.

In the context of distribution, quantum computing holds the promise of optimizing warehouse operations. For instance, it could calculate the optimal packing arrangements for pallets or containers, maximizing space utilization and minimizing shipping costs. Moreover, it could model complex scenarios to streamline the flow of goods through a distribution center, ensuring that each item is stored and retrieved in the most efficient manner possible.

Python's role in this quantum leap is instrumental. The language's flexibility and the development of quantum programming libraries such as Qiskit allow researchers and practitioners to experiment with quantum algorithms even before widespread access to quantum computers becomes available. Through these tools, supply chain professionals can begin to understand and prepare for the integration of quantum computing into their operations.

1. **Superior Problem-Solving**: Tackling multi-variable problems like global supply chain optimization becomes feasible, leading to unprecedented levels of efficiency.

2. **Risk Management**: Quantum computing can simulate

complex risk scenarios in seconds, enabling companies to better prepare for and mitigate potential disruptions.

3. **Market Responsiveness**: The ability to rapidly reconfigure supply chains in response to market changes can provide a competitive edge in today's volatile business environment.

4. **Innovation in Logistics**: New quantum-based algorithms could lead to the development of novel logistics services and products.

5. **Cost Reduction**: Although quantum computing requires significant investment, the long-term cost savings through optimized operations could be substantial.

However, embracing quantum computing is not without its hurdles. The technology is still in its nascent stages, and practical, scalable quantum computers are not yet widely available. The skill set required to develop and implement quantum algorithms is highly specialized, suggesting a steep learning curve for supply chain professionals. Furthermore, the implications for data security are profound, as quantum computers have the potential to break current encryption methods, necessitating the development of quantum-resistant cybersecurity measures.

As quantum computing continues to evolve, its confluence with supply chain analytics is inevitable. It presents an exciting future where the boundaries of logistics and distribution are pushed to new horizons, and the mastery of quantum algorithms could become as pivotal to supply chain professionals as Lean principles are today.

In conclusion, while quantum computing remains in the

experimental phase, its eventual maturation will herald a transformative impact on supply chain logistics and distribution. As this technology develops, it behooves supply chain leaders to monitor advancements and prepare for the quantum revolution that promises to reshape the industry in ways we are only beginning to imagine.

CHAPTER 10:
IMPLEMENTING
ANALYTICS PROJECTS
IN SUPPLY CHAINS

Developing a Supply Chain Analytics Strategy

I n the orchestration of supply chain operations, an analytics strategy serves as the conductor's baton, directing the flow and tempo of a company's logistical symphony. The development of a supply chain analytics strategy is a meticulous process that involves the alignment of data-driven insights with business objectives to enhance decision-making and operational efficiency.

The initial step in crafting a robust analytics strategy is the articulation of clear and measurable goals that resonate with the overarching business objectives. Whether the aim is to reduce costs, improve service levels, or enhance supplier relationships, the strategy must encapsulate these targets within its framework. A well-defined strategy is akin to a roadmap; it guides the organization through the complex landscape of data collection, analysis, and application.

Subsequently, the identification of key performance indicators (KPIs) is integral to the strategy. KPIs act as beacons, illuminating the path to success by providing quantifiable metrics that gauge the effectiveness of supply chain operations. With the right KPIs in place, an organization can monitor progress, identify areas of improvement, and pivot strategies in real-time.

At the heart of a supply chain analytics strategy lies the aggregation and integration of relevant data. Data sources can be diverse, ranging from internal systems such as enterprise resource planning (ERP) and warehouse management systems (WMS) to external sources including market data and supplier information. The strategy must encompass methods for consolidating these data streams to paint a comprehensive picture of the supply chain.

Python's prowess in handling data makes it an indispensable tool for implementing a supply chain analytics strategy. With libraries such as pandas for data manipulation and scikit-learn for machine learning, Python enables supply chain analysts to cleanse, process, and analyze vast datasets. The language's versatility allows for the creation of predictive models that can forecast demand, optimize stock levels, and preempt bottlenecks in the supply chain.

In addition to data handling, the strategy should incorporate advanced analytics methodologies. Techniques such as predictive analytics can forecast future trends based on historical data, while prescriptive analytics can suggest the best course of action when faced with different scenarios. These methodologies empower organizations to move from a reactive to a proactive stance in their supply chain operations.

Another cornerstone of a supply chain analytics strategy is the establishment of robust data governance practices. Data governance ensures the accuracy, consistency, and security of data, which is particularly crucial when making data-informed decisions. A sound data governance framework mitigates the risk of data breaches and ensures compliance with regulations, thus safeguarding the company's reputation and competitive advantage.

To ensure the successful deployment of the analytics strategy, the organization must also cultivate a culture that values data-driven decision-making. This involves training and empowering employees with the skills to interpret analytics and make informed decisions. It is a shift from intuition-based to evidence-based management, where every link in the supply chain is underpinned by data insights.

Lastly, the strategy must be scalable and flexible to adapt to the evolving technological landscape and business environment. As new technologies emerge, such as artificial intelligence (AI) and the Internet of Things (IoT), the analytics strategy should offer the agility to integrate these advancements and leverage them for enhanced supply chain performance.

Developing a supply chain analytics strategy is not a one-time endeavor but an ongoing process of refinement and evolution. It requires a forward-thinking mindset that embraces innovation and continuous improvement. By laying down a solid analytical foundation, organizations can navigate the complexities of the supply chain with greater confidence, agility, and insight, driving them towards a future of unrivaled operational excellence.

In sum, a supply chain analytics strategy is the blueprint for harnessing data's transformative power, unlocking opportunities for optimization, and fostering an environment where every decision is informed by insights and geared towards achieving strategic business outcomes.

Project Management Frameworks for SC Analytics

A harmonious fusion of meticulous planning and agile execution, project management frameworks are the scaffolding upon which successful supply chain analytics initiatives are built. These frameworks provide a structured approach to managing complex projects, ensuring that analytics endeavors are completed on time, within budget, and to the desired quality standards.

One of the pivotal frameworks in this realm is the Project Management Institute's (PMI) Project Management Body of Knowledge (PMBOK), which outlines a set of standard terminologies and guidelines for project management. PMBOK's process groups—initiating, planning, executing, monitoring and controlling, and closing—offer a comprehensive methodology for overseeing analytics projects from inception to fruition.

The initiating process group begins with the identification of the project's purpose and feasibility. It involves defining the scope of the analytics project, recognizing its objectives and deliverables, and securing the necessary approvals to move forward. This phase sets the foundation for the project by ensuring that there is a clear understanding of what needs to be achieved and why.

In the planning process group, the focus shifts to developing a robust project plan. This encompasses establishing the project's timeline, resources, and budget. For supply chain analytics projects, this also includes selecting the appropriate data sources, analytics tools, and methodologies that will be used. Python, with its extensive libraries for data analysis, may be chosen as the primary tool for data manipulation and model development. Detailed planning also involves risk management —identifying potential obstacles and devising strategies to mitigate them.

The executing process group is where the project plan is put into action. In the context of supply chain analytics, this could involve collecting and cleansing data, developing predictive models, or implementing machine learning algorithms. Throughout this phase, effective communication and stakeholder engagement are crucial to ensure alignment and buy-in from all parties involved.

Monitoring and controlling process group involves tracking the project's progress against the plan, ensuring that the project remains on course. Key performance indicators and milestones are used to measure progress. In supply chain analytics, this could involve assessing the accuracy of predictive models or the efficiency gains from optimized routes. Adjustments are made as needed to correct deviations from the plan, and quality control ensures that the project's outputs meet the required standards.

The closing process group signifies the completion of the project. It includes the formal acceptance of the project deliverables and the release of project resources. Lessons learned are documented to inform future projects, and a post-implementation review may be conducted to evaluate the project's success and the effectiveness of the analytics solutions deployed.

Another influential framework is Agile, which emphasizes flexibility, collaboration, and customer feedback. Agile methodologies, such as Scrum or Kanban, are particularly well-suited for analytics projects where requirements may change rapidly, and incremental progress is favored over a single, final deliverable. In an Agile environment, supply chain analytics projects benefit from iterative development, allowing for continuous refinement of models and strategies based on real-time feedback and changing market conditions.

For supply chain analytics projects, a hybrid approach that combines the structured rigor of PMBOK with the flexibility of Agile practices is often most effective. This blended framework allows for comprehensive planning and control while retaining the adaptability needed to respond to dynamic supply chain challenges.

Project management frameworks are not just administrative tools; they are strategic assets that, when applied effectively, can enhance the success rate of supply chain analytics projects. By providing a clear structure for project execution, these frameworks enable supply chain managers to navigate the complexities of analytics initiatives, driving towards insights that optimize supply chain performance and deliver substantial business value.

In the realm of supply chain analytics, where data is plentiful and the potential for optimization is vast, robust project management frameworks are the linchpin that ensures initiatives are not only envisioned but also meticulously executed and brought to successful completion.

Data Science Skills and Team Building

In the heart of every formidable supply chain analytics initiative lies a team of skilled professionals, each member a vital cog in the intricate machinery of data-driven decision-making. The cultivation of a proficient team is a deliberate and thoughtful process, one that requires an acute understanding of the multifaceted nature of data science and the diverse competencies that it encompasses.

The cornerstone of an effective supply chain analytics team is a solid foundation in data science skills. These skills range from statistical analysis and machine learning to data wrangling and visualization. Mastery in programming languages such as Python is crucial, as it serves as the key to unlocking the power of analytics. With Python's extensive libraries like Pandas for data manipulation, NumPy for numerical computing, and Matplotlib for visualization, team members can adeptly handle the vast datasets characteristic of supply chain systems.

Beyond technical prowess, the ability to translate complex data insights into actionable business strategies is what sets apart a good data science team from a great one. This translational skill requires an intimate knowledge of the supply chain domain, as well as the acumen to discern patterns and trends that can lead to significant operational improvements. For instance, a data scientist might use a Python-based forecasting model to predict inventory levels, but it is their understanding of supply chain dynamics that allows them to recommend strategic adjustments to inventory policy.

Constructing such a team begins with identifying the roles that will form the backbone of the analytics department. Data scientists bring the analytical horsepower, while data engineers ensure the smooth flow and accessibility of data. Business analysts bridge the gap between technical solutions and business needs, and project managers oversee the orchestration of analytics projects, ensuring they align with strategic business objectives.

The selection process for these roles involves not only vetting candidates for their technical capabilities but also for their collaborative spirit and adaptability. The dynamic nature of supply chains demands professionals who can pivot swiftly in response to emerging trends or disruptions.

Once assembled, fostering collaboration and continuous learning within the team is paramount. Regular knowledge-sharing sessions can help keep the team abreast of the latest developments in the field, from advancements in AI algorithms to novel applications of data analytics in supply chain management. These sessions can take the form of code reviews, where team members critique and improve upon Python scripts, or collaborative workshops, where they tackle complex supply chain problems together.

In addition to internal team development, forging connections with other departments such as IT, operations, and finance is essential. These cross-functional collaborations enrich the analytics team's perspective and ensure that the insights generated are embedded across the organization's fabric.

Team-building in the realm of supply chain analytics is not a one-off event but a continuous endeavor. It requires nurturing an environment that values curiosity, encourages experimentation, and rewards innovation. It is through this environment that the analytics team becomes more than the sum of its parts, driving forward the organization's supply chain capabilities with precision and insight.

The integration of data science skills within a well-structured team is a critical asset for any organization looking to leverage supply chain analytics. It is this blend of individual expertise and collective synergy that enables the seamless transformation of raw data into a strategic powerhouse, fueling smarter, faster, and more efficient supply chain decisions.

Change Management and Organizational Culture

Embarking on the path to establishing a data-centric supply chain requires not just technological shifts, but also an evolution in organizational culture and behavior. The journey of integrating supply chain analytics within a company's operations is as much about managing change as it is about managing data. It is a transformative process that demands a strategic approach to change management, underpinned by a supportive organizational culture.

The bedrock of successful change management in the context of supply chain analytics is a clear vision. Leaders must articulate a compelling future state where data-driven insights lead to enhanced decision-making and competitive advantage. Envisioning this future state involves a comprehensive understanding of how supply chain analytics can reshape operational efficiencies, customer experiences, and ultimately, financial performance.

To move towards this vision, change must be meticulously planned and executed. This begins with a thorough assessment of the current organizational culture and its readiness for change. Are teams accustomed to making decisions based on data, or do they rely on intuition and experience? Is there a culture of continuous improvement and learning, or do resistance and complacency dominate? Answering such questions helps in identifying potential barriers and designing strategies to overcome them.

One of the most effective strategies in the arsenal of change management is communication. Transparent and consistent messaging about the benefits of supply chain analytics, the changes it will bring, and the support available for employees during the transition is vital. It is crucial to tailor this communication to different levels within the organization, from executives to front-line staff, ensuring that everyone understands their role in the evolution.

Training and education form the backbone of this cultural shift. Developing a curriculum that covers the essentials of supply chain analytics, from understanding data ecosystems to applying machine learning models, is critical. Employees should be able to access hands-on training with tools like Python's Scikit-learn for machine learning or TensorFlow for deep learning, providing them with practical skills they can apply in their roles.

In tandem with training, establishing a 'data analytics champion' within each department can accelerate the cultural transformation. These champions can serve as the point of contact for their teams' analytics needs, liaise with the data science team, and help embed data-driven practices within their workflows.

Leadership, too, plays a pivotal role in fostering an analytics-centric culture. Leaders must lead by example, using data to inform their decisions and encouraging their teams to do the same. They should celebrate successes achieved through analytics and recognize those who contribute to these wins, thereby reinforcing the value of data-driven decision-making.

However, the shift to a data-centric culture is not without its challenges. Resistance to change is a natural human tendency, and it can manifest in various forms, from skepticism about data accuracy to fear of job displacement. Addressing these concerns directly, providing reassurance, and demonstrating the positive impacts of analytics on job roles can help mitigate resistance.

Change management for supply chain analytics is an ongoing process. It requires continuous monitoring, feedback, and iteration. As the organization evolves, so too must its approach to managing change. This might involve adapting training programs to address new competencies, updating communication strategies to reflect the growing maturity of analytics usage, or revising incentives to align with the desired data-driven behaviors.

Ultimately, the integration of supply chain analytics into an organization's fabric is a complex yet rewarding endeavor. It necessitates a cultural metamorphosis where data becomes a cornerstone of every decision, and where continuous improvement through analytics becomes the norm. By managing change effectively and fostering an organizational culture that embraces data, companies can unlock the full potential of their supply chains, ensuring resilience, agility, and sustained competitive advantage in the ever-evolving business landscape.

Partnerships and Collaboration with Tech Providers

In the digitally interconnected world of supply chains,

the creation and maintenance of robust partnerships with technology providers are indispensable. These collaborations can significantly amplify a company's ability to leverage analytics for deeper insights and more effective decision-making. The synergy between supply chain enterprises and tech providers is a catalyst for innovation and operational excellence.

Forming strategic alliances with technology vendors enables organizations to tap into advanced analytical tools and platforms without the prohibitive cost and time associated with in-house development. These partnerships offer access to cutting-edge technologies such as cloud computing, machine learning algorithms, and artificial intelligence, which are pivotal in extracting valuable insights from complex supply chain data.

The selection of tech providers should be a deliberate process, grounded in the organization's specific needs and strategic goals. It is essential to identify partners who not only offer the requisite technological expertise but also share a commitment to the company's vision for data-driven transformation. The criteria for selection often extend beyond the technical capabilities to include factors such as provider reputation, support structures, and the potential for long-term collaboration.

Once chosen, forging a collaborative relationship with these providers is a multifaceted endeavor. It necessitates clear communication of objectives, expectations, and the scope of the partnership. Regular interactions and joint planning sessions are crucial to align the technology solutions with the organization's supply chain analytics strategy. This collaborative planning also helps in identifying potential integration challenges early on and developing contingency plans to address them.

Collaboration with tech providers is not merely transactional; it should be viewed as a partnership in the truest sense. Engaging in knowledge sharing and joint innovation efforts can lead to the co-creation of customized solutions that precisely address the unique challenges and opportunities within the supply chain. It also allows for the pooling of resources and expertise, which can accelerate the development of new capabilities and the adoption of best practices in analytics.

The integration of external technologies into the organization's supply chain operations must be handled with meticulous care. It involves technical considerations such as compatibility with existing systems, data security protocols, and scalability. Additionally, there is a human element to this integration, requiring the involvement and buy-in of the personnel who will utilize these technologies in their daily operations.

Training and support are fundamental to the successful adoption of technologies provided by external partners. Ensuring that staff have the necessary skills to harness these tools effectively is critical. Tech providers should offer comprehensive training programs and user-friendly documentation to facilitate a smooth transition. Ongoing support, whether in the form of help desks, user communities, or dedicated account managers, is also vital to ensuring that any issues are promptly addressed, and users feel confident in leveraging the technology to its full potential.

Evaluating the performance of technology partnerships is an ongoing process. It involves setting measurable objectives and key performance indicators that reflect the value and impact of the collaboration on supply chain analytics initiatives. Regular reviews of the partnership's outcomes help in determining its effectiveness and identifying areas for improvement or expansion.

In summary, partnerships and collaborations with technology providers are not an optional luxury but a strategic necessity in the realm of supply chain analytics. They bring a wealth of specialized knowledge, innovative solutions, and support structures that can dramatically enhance an organization's analytics capabilities. By carefully selecting the right partners and fostering a collaborative relationship built on mutual goals and trust, supply chain enterprises can realize the transformative power of analytics and stay ahead in the competitive landscape.

Proof of Concept and Pilot Programs

The implementation of supply chain analytics often begins with the development of a proof of concept (PoC) or pilot program. These preliminary stages serve as a litmus test for the feasibility and effectiveness of a proposed analytics solution before its full-scale deployment. They are a prudent step in mitigating risk and validating that the solution aligns with the organization's operational requirements and strategic objectives.

Proof of concept is a targeted exercise designed to demonstrate whether a particular analytics application has the potential to solve a specific business problem. It is a controlled and cost-effective way to explore the viability of new ideas without committing extensive resources. A successful PoC provides tangible evidence of the solution's capabilities and helps secure stakeholder buy-in by showcasing the potential benefits in a real-world scenario.

Pilot programs take the concept a step further by implementing the analytics solution in a limited area of the business. The scope of a pilot is broader than a PoC and is intended to replicate the conditions of full deployment on a smaller scale. This approach allows the organization to test the solution within its own ecosystem, examining the practical aspects of integration, user adoption, and impact on existing processes.

Both PoCs and pilot programs are instrumental in gathering valuable insights into the technical performance and user acceptance of analytics solutions. They provide an opportunity to identify any unforeseen challenges, such as data quality issues, system incompatibilities, or resistance to change among the workforce. Addressing these issues at an early stage can save considerable time and expense down the line.

A structured methodology is critical for the success of PoCs and pilot programs. It begins with the clear definition of objectives and success criteria, which should be directly linked to the business outcomes the solution is expected to influence. Stakeholders from relevant departments must be involved from the outset to ensure alignment with business needs and to foster a sense of ownership over the project.

During the PoC or pilot, data collection and analysis play an essential role. Metrics and key performance indicators (KPIs) should be established to measure the solution's performance against the defined goals. Regular monitoring and assessment of these metrics help in understanding the effectiveness of the solution and guide any necessary adjustments.

Documentation of the process and findings is another key aspect. Detailed records not only provide a basis for evaluating the PoC or pilot but also create a knowledge base for scaling the solution. These records should include technical configurations, user feedback, performance data, and lessons learned.

Upon completion of the PoC or pilot, a thorough review should be conducted to determine the next steps. If the results are positive and the solution is deemed a good fit, the organization can proceed with confidence to broader implementation. Conversely, if the solution falls short of expectations, the findings can inform the decision to revise the approach or explore alternative solutions.

In the context of supply chain analytics, PoCs and pilot programs are indispensable tools for innovation. They encourage experimentation and learning by providing a sandbox environment where new technologies and methodologies can be tested without significant risk. By proving the value of analytics initiatives in a tangible, controlled setting, PoCs and pilot programs pave the way for transformative change and continuous improvement within the supply chain.

Scaling Analytics Solutions across the Enterprise

Scaling an analytics solution across an entire enterprise is akin to orchestrating a complex symphony. Every instrument, every note, must harmonize perfectly to create an impactful performance. In the realm of supply chain analytics, this means expanding the proven capabilities of pilot programs to the full breadth of the organization—transforming isolated successes into widespread benefits.

Scaling involves extending the analytics solution beyond the controlled environments of PoCs and pilot programs to the diverse and often unpredictable landscape of the entire enterprise. This requires meticulous planning, robust infrastructure, and a company-wide change management initiative. It is a critical transition, where strategic insights become deeply embedded into daily operations, decision-making processes, and organizational culture.

The journey of scaling begins with a comprehensive assessment of the technological foundations. The infrastructure must be resilient, capable of handling an increased volume and velocity of data from various sources. It should also be flexible enough to accommodate future growth and technological advancements. Cloud-based platforms are frequently at the core of such scalable systems, offering the elasticity and agility needed for expansion.

Another cornerstone of scaling is the standardization of processes and analytics models. Consistency in data handling, analysis, and reporting ensures that insights are reliable and comparable across different departments and geographies. Standardization also streamlines training and support activities, as employees across the organization encounter a uniform analytical environment.

Crucial to the success of scaling is the alignment with the organization's strategic goals. Analytics should not be an afterthought but a driving force behind achieving business objectives. This alignment ensures that the scaled solutions contribute value and remain relevant as corporate strategies evolve.

Change management cannot be overstated when it comes to scaling analytics solutions. The human element—how employees interact with new systems, interpret data, and make decisions based on analytics—is often the most challenging aspect of scaling. A proactive approach to change management involves clear communication of the benefits, comprehensive training programs, and ongoing support to encourage adoption.

Furthermore, governance structures must be in place to oversee the scaled operations. Governance provides clarity on roles and responsibilities, enforces data security and privacy policies, and sets the stage for continuous improvement through regular reviews and updates to the analytics solutions.

A phased approach to scaling can help manage risks and allow for iterative learning and adaptation. Starting with a single department or business unit and progressively expanding to others enables the organization to refine the process, building on the successes and learnings from each phase.

Throughout the scaling process, measurement and analysis of impact are paramount. Organizations must track the same metrics and KPIs established during the pilot phase but now at a larger scale. This not only demonstrates the value of the analytics initiatives but also highlights areas for further optimization.

Finally, fostering a culture of data-driven decision-making is essential. As analytics become more integrated into the enterprise, every employee should be empowered to leverage data insights. This cultural shift is a significant indicator of a successful scale-up—an enterprise where data analytics is not just a tool but a fundamental component of the business fabric.

Scaling analytics solutions across the enterprise is a transformative process that positions organizations to unlock the full potential of their data. With a strategic, structured approach, businesses can turn the harmony of individual successes into a powerful concert that reverberates throughout the supply chain, driving efficiency, innovation, and competitive advantage.

Measuring Success and ROI of Analytics Projects

In the pursuit of excellence within the sphere of supply chain analytics, the critical yardstick for evaluating the triumph of any analytics undertaking is the measurement of its success and the return on investment (ROI). It is not simply about the implementation of sophisticated algorithms or the accumulation of vast datasets, but rather the tangible outcomes that these efforts engender. This scrutiny is vital, as it quantifies the value analytics projects add to an organization.

Measuring success and ROI involves the meticulous analysis of both qualitative and quantitative benefits derived from analytics projects. It is the compass that guides enterprises, indicating whether they are on the correct path towards achieving their strategic objectives or if course corrections are necessary. The process of measurement is multifaceted, requiring a clear understanding of the initial goals, the investment of resources, and the net gains achieved.

Quantitatively, ROI is calculated by considering the total benefits—such as cost reductions, increased efficiency, and revenue growth—against the total costs, including technology investments, human capital, and operational changes. This calculation should span not just the immediate aftermath of project implementation but also the long-term effects that ripple through the supply chain.

For instance, an analytics project aimed at optimizing inventory levels can lead to reduced holding costs, minimized stockouts, and improved cash flow. These outcomes must be translated into financial metrics that reflect the monetary impact on the organization. A positive ROI is indicative of a project that has successfully translated data insights into economic value.

Qualitative measures, on the other hand, assess the non-monetary impact, such as enhanced customer satisfaction, better decision-making capabilities, and improved supplier relationships. These aspects may be harder to quantify but are no less significant, as they can lead to sustained competitive advantage and brand loyalty. An effective way to capture qualitative outcomes is through feedback surveys, customer satisfaction scores, and employee engagement metrics.

Benchmarking against industry standards and best practices can provide additional context to the success of analytics projects. It allows an organization to gauge its performance relative to peers and to strive for continuous improvement. Benchmarking also uncovers gaps in capabilities and identifies opportunities for further enhancements.

Critical to the measurement process is the establishment of clear, relevant KPIs before the commencement of an analytics project. These KPIs must align with the strategic goals of the organization and should be designed to capture the specific improvements expected from the project. Examples include improved forecast accuracy, reduced lead times, or increased order fulfillment rates.

Regular monitoring and reporting of these KPIs create transparency and accountability. It enables stakeholders to track progress and make informed decisions about the future direction of analytics initiatives. It also fosters a culture of performance where the value of analytics is recognized and celebrated.

Beyond the initial measurement, organizations should also consider the scalability and sustainability of analytics projects. The long-term ROI is significantly influenced by how well the analytics solutions adapt to changing market conditions and business needs. A project that may have a high ROI in the short term but requires constant, costly updates may not be as valuable in the long run.

Furthermore, the integration of learnings from each project into the overall analytics strategy can compound the ROI over time. Lessons learned should be documented and shared, serving as a repository of knowledge that can inform future projects and strategies.

Measuring success and ROI is an ongoing imperative in the lifecycle of supply chain analytics projects. It provides clarity on the effectiveness and efficiency of investments, reinforces the strategic alignment of analytics initiatives, and celebrates the achievements of data-driven decision-making. In a world of ever-increasing complexity, the ability to demonstrate the value of analytics is not just beneficial; it is essential for the sustainable growth and evolution of an enterprise.

Future Skills and Competency Development in Supply Chain Analytics

The advancing frontier of supply chain analytics not only demands cutting-edge technology but also a workforce with the skills to harness its full potential. Future-proofing an organization hinges on its ability to cultivate a culture of continuous learning and capacity building.

The core of competency development lies in a deep understanding of data—its acquisition, cleansing, exploration, and analysis. Proficiency in programming languages such as Python is increasingly indispensable, as it enables professionals to manipulate large datasets and apply statistical models. For example, writing a Python script to automate the cleaning of shipment data can significantly reduce the time spent on manual data entry, allowing analysts to focus on higher-level tasks.

Beyond technical skills, the ability to interpret and communicate insights gleaned from data is equally vital. Data visualization tools such as Tableau or Power BI come into play, transforming complex data sets into intuitive dashboards and reports. This empowers decision-makers to grasp key trends and patterns at a glance, facilitating more informed strategic choices.

Increasingly, machine learning and AI are making their mark on supply chain analytics, necessitating a grasp of these technologies. Understanding algorithms and their applications, such as using neural networks for demand forecasting, equips professionals with the means to drive innovation and efficiency. However, the implementation of these advanced tools requires a blend of technical know-how and strategic thinking to ensure they align with business objectives and add tangible value.

Another emerging area is the integration of blockchain technology for enhancing traceability and security in supply chains. Learning how this technology can be leveraged to create immutable records of transactions and streamline operations is becoming an essential competency in certain sectors.

The human element of supply chain analytics must not be overshadowed by technological prowess. Soft skills such as leadership, collaboration, and problem-solving are the glue that holds analytics initiatives together. A culture of teamwork and the ability to lead cross-functional projects are critical for driving change and ensuring that data-driven strategies are effectively implemented.

Risk management is also becoming a more pronounced aspect of supply chain analytics. Professionals must be equipped to identify potential risks, assess their impact, and develop mitigation strategies. This includes not just operational risks but also ethical considerations, such as ensuring AI applications do not inadvertently lead to biased outcomes.

Finally, a commitment to ethical data practices and an understanding of privacy laws and regulations round out the skillset for supply chain analytics professionals. As data becomes an increasingly valuable commodity, the responsibility to manage it ethically and transparently is paramount.

In conclusion, the future of supply chain analytics rests on a foundation of advanced technical skills, enriched by strategic insight, leadership qualities, and a steadfast commitment to ethical practices. Developing these competencies is not a one-time event but a continual journey of growth and adaptation. As organizations invest in these areas, they pave the way for a more dynamic, resilient, and competitive presence in the global marketplace. The path forward is clear: to thrive in the world of supply chain analytics, one must embrace both the technological and the human aspects, fostering a learning environment that evolves in tandem with the industry's demands.

ADDITIONAL RESOURCES

In order to further enhance your understanding and skills in the field of Supply Chain Analytics, the following resources are highly recommended. These resources have been carefully selected to provide a comprehensive and multi-faceted learning experience, complementing the material covered in "Supply Chain Analytics."

Books

1. **"Supply Chain Management: Strategy, Planning, and Operation" by Sunil Chopra and Peter Meindl**
   - A foundational text offering extensive insights into the strategic and operational aspects of supply chain management.

2. **"Data Science for Supply Chain Forecasting" by Nicolas Vandeput**
   - This book focuses on applying data science techniques for more accurate and efficient supply chain forecasting.

3. **"Lean Six Sigma for Supply Chain Management" by James William Martin**
   - A practical guide to employing Lean Six Sigma principles to optimize supply chain processes and enhance efficiency.

Online Courses

1. **MITx's MicroMasters Program in Supply Chain Management (edX)**
   - A series of graduate-level courses designed to provide advanced, professional, graduate-level foundation in Supply Chain Management.

2. **Supply Chain Analytics Essentials (Coursera)**
   - Offers an introduction to the fundamental concepts of supply chain analytics in an interactive online format.

Journals and Publications

1. **"Journal of Supply Chain Management"**
   - A leading academic journal offering the latest research and developments in the field.

2. **"Supply Chain Management Review"**
   - Provides case studies, reports, and analyses on various aspects of supply chain management.

Websites and Online Resources

1. **Supply Chain Digest**
   - An online portal offering news, opinion pieces, and educational materials on supply chain management and logistics.

2. **SCM World**
   - A global community of supply chain practitioners, offering webinars, reports, and events.

Professional Organizations

1. **Council of Supply Chain Management Professionals (CSCMP)**
   - Offers networking opportunities, training, and certifications in supply chain management.

2. **Institute for Supply Management (ISM)**
    ◦ Provides resources, educational materials, and certification programs for supply chain professionals.

Conferences and Workshops

1. **APICS Conferences**
    ◦ Annual conferences providing insights, research, and networking opportunities in the world of supply chain and operations management.

2. **Gartner Supply Chain Symposium/Xpo**
    ◦ A premier event for supply chain leaders, offering strategic advice and practical supply chain management insights.

www.ingramcontent.com/pod-product-compliance
Lightning Source LLC
Chambersburg PA
CBHW071107050326
40690CB00008B/1146